GARLAND STUDIES ON

THE ELDERLY IN AMERICA

edited by
STUART BRUCHEY
UNIVERSITY OF MAINE

A GARLAND SERIES

CARING FOR ELDERLY PARENTS

THE RELATIONSHIP BETWEEN STRESS AND CHOICE

MARLA BERG-WEGER

GARLAND PUBLISHING, INC.
NEW YORK & LONDON / 1996

Library of Congress Cataloging-in-Publication Data

Berg-Weger, Marla, 1956–
    Caring for elderly parents : the relationship between stress
and choice / Marla Berg-Weger.
        p.   cm. — (Garland studies on the elderly in America)
    Includes bibliographical references and index.
    ISBN 0-8153-2401-4 (alk. paper)
    1. Aging parent—Home care—Psychological aspects. 2.
Caregivers—Psychology. 3. Daughters—Psychology. 4. Parent
and adult child. 5. Stress (Psychology) I. Title. II. Series.
HV1451.B49 1996
362.6—dc20   96-821

Printed on acid-free, 250-year-life paper
Manufactured in the United States of America

To Jim, Cameron and Lauren who teach me about life

Contents

List of Tables

Acknowledgments

To all the families who devote themselves tirelessly and with compassion in providing care to their parents, I extend my appreciation and respect. In particular, I would like to recognize those caregivers who contributed to this research. Their willingness to share their caregiving experience enables researchers and practitioners to gain a better understanding of who they are and how they move through the process of caregiving.

I would also like to acknowledge the valuable contributions of my mentors and colleagues. It is the support of these professionals that inspires me in my appreciation and mastery of the art of the research.

Preface

This book is an exploration of the relationships adult daughters have with their elderly parents. The family caregiving literature includes a rich and extensive body of knowledge regarding issues related to the identity of caregivers, the type of care that is provided and the effects of the caregiving experience for the caregiver and the care-recipient. However, scholars have less frequently studied the phase of the caregiving experience which precedes the actual onset of caregiving responsibilities. This scholarly endeavor is an attempt to examine that phase of the caregiver-elder relationship which determines the identity of the caregiver and the impact of that decision-making process on the caregiver herself.

My interest in this area of study grew from my social work practice with family caregivers in a multidisciplinary geriatric assessment clinic. Throughout the time I spent working with this population, I found my curiosity growing around issues related to family decision-making regarding care of the elderly parent. I began to inquire how the family member who had accompanied the elder to the clinic had been "elected" to the role of the primary caregiver. I found the responses fascinating, thus beginning my own exploration into this area.

Caring for Elderly Parents

I

Introduction and Overview

INTRODUCTION

Caregiving to the elderly has been occurring, in some form, within the family in a quiet, nonmonetized, nontechnological manner for centuries. It has come to be viewed as a private function of family life, usually performed by few persons (typically one) with little fanfare and out of the mainstream of the public eye (Hooyman 1989). Families provide nearly 80% of the informal home-based care provided to frail, elderly relatives (Horowitz 1985; National Center for Health Statistics 1975). Fewer than 10% of elders receive care from formal sources, while approximately 75% receive care exclusively from informal sources (Doty 1986; Stone, Cafferata & Sangl 1987).

While it is recognized that most families care for their elders, little attention has been devoted to examining how non-spouse family members are selected to serve as caregivers or the potential impact of the selection process on the elder or family. Much is assumed about the ways family caregivers are inducted into the role. Families, however, engage in a decision-making process regarding "caregiving alternatives" which has seldom been studied (Horowitz, 1985a, 227).

The decisions made regarding care provision can be complex and difficult. Guberman, Maheu and Maille (1992, 615) note "the process leading to a decision to assume caregiving is never a result of one and the same factor." It is important to examine the onset of the caregiving relationship to gain insight into how the induction factors "inter-relate and mutually reinforce one another and in what conditions and situations they emerge" (Guberman, et al. 1992, 616).

Study is needed to examine the relationship between induction and caregiving outcomes for the caregiver, particularly adult children, as researchers have not typically viewed this group at risk for negative outcomes (Bowers 1987) nor have the factors that place caregivers in jeopardy for negative outcomes been fully examined (Chesla, Martinson & Muwaswes 1994). It is important to understand the relationship between caregiver induction factors and caregiver strain,

3

as most strain studies have focused on only those caregiver factors which occur post-induction. Caregiver role induction may be a characteristic of the caregiver (by choice, position in the family, gender or available resources, for example), and as noted by Pearlin and colleagues "virtually everything we are interested in learning about caregiving and its consequences is potentially influenced by key characteristics of the caregiver" (Pearlin, Mullan, Semple & Skaff 1990, 585). Caregiver strain can result from factors related to caregiver status. Examining the events and perceptions which occur prior to the onset of the caregiving relationship may provide insight into the sources of caregiver strain and appropriate coping strategies. Gaining insight into how induction factors relate to caregiver strain can aid program planners and practitioners in identifying and intervening with caregivers, families and elders at risk for poor outcome.

The Caregiving Role

Caregiving may be considered a role, as those who engage in it seem to identify themselves with the tasks involved. Role is broadly defined as "a pattern of behavior that is characteristic or expected of an individual occupying a particular position within the social system" (Wolman 1989, 297) and further defined as "those presentations of self that we all assume in social or work situations" which are "temporary or limited, and are consciously and deliberately assumed" (Karpel & Strauss 1983, 26). Family roles are "more permanent, less flexible and usually less conscious" (Karpel & Strauss 1983, 26).

Roles can be prescribed (assigned by the social system) or ascribed (achieved) and are usually complementary (Compton & Galaway 1979, 86–87). Role expectations are determined or confirmed by the social system and may conflict with individual role expectations. The more an individual feels forced into a role, the greater the likelihood of role conflict or incongruity. Role incongruity is the conflict between individual and social system role expectations (Compton & Galaway 1979).

Family caregiving of the elderly may be defined as "one or more family members giving aid or assistance to other family members beyond that required as part of normal everyday life" which is a result of a need by the elder on another individual for "activity essential for daily living" (Walker, Pratt & Eddy 1995, 402–403). Conceptualization of family caregiving has been difficult to capture as the phenomena has traditionally been defined within the context of gender-specific (female) terms (Walker, et al. 1995).

Caregiver Role Induction

The process by which the caregiver assumes the caregiving role is referred to as caregiver induction. Caregiver induction is defined here as the process by which a person who has heretofore not provided care assumes a role and a role identity associated with providing care to an elderly family member. Induction into a family role occurs in various ways but often in response to individual or family need (Karpel & Strauss 1983). Walker and colleagues further define the inception of caregiving occcurring ". . . when aging family members require assistance due to debilitating chronic conditions or diseases. . ." (Walker, et al. 1995, 402).

Regarding role induction in general, Orlinsky and Howard (1978, 308) suggest "the relationship is born when its participants begin to associate with one another, grows as the pattern of the association evolves, and survives only so long as they have contact." While families usually have established relationships, the caregiving relationship with the elder is formed when a member begins to perform acts for an elder unable to do so independently. The caregiving relationship may change in response to elder need and is maintained as long as need exists and the caregiver is able to fulfill the role.

Caregiver Strain

Caregivers can experience both distress and growth as they attempt to adapt to new roles and expectations (Masciocchi, Thomas & Moeller 1984). Caregiving can overwhelm coping resources (Lazarus & Folkman 1984). The act of providing care to an elderly family member requires the caregiver to assume a role for which he/she may be unprepared (Masiocchi, et al. 1984). Assuming the caregiving role may require the caregiver to alter his or her perception of a previously close or reciprocal relationship and can also lead to "an extraordinary and unequally distributed burden" (Pearlin, et al. 1990, 583).

OVERVIEW OF THE PROPOSED STUDY

The purpose of this study is to build on existing knowledge regarding factors related to caregiver strain. Empirical evidence has established links between such caregiver factors as age, race, marital status, relationship to elder, duration of caregiving, socioeconomic status and physical proximity and caregiver strain. This study will attempt to further understanding of caregiver strain by examining relationships between two caregiver induction factors and strain. The induction factors to be examined are: 1) level of willingness to assume the role and 2) reasons for caregiver selection.

Two theoretical perspectives are used to inform the research questions for this study. Role theory is used to establish caregiving as a normative role in the life cycle and explain the relationship between role assumption, level of willingness and caregiver strain. Social exchange theory is used to understand caregiver selection by identifying reasons for selection. This theory further explains caregiver strain by identifying differences in the reasons caregivers are selected for the role. This study can further our knowledge of caregiver strain by adding explanatory variables relating to caregiver induction. Caregiver level of willingness to assume the role and reasons for selection are seldom examined and warrant study as factors associated with caregiver strain. The relationship between these two induction factors, level of willingness and reasons for selection, and caregiver strain will be examined multivariately. Caregiving factors previously associated with caregiver strain will be controlled in this analysis as empirical evidence is sufficient to suggest a causal relationship between these factors and caregiver strain.

II
The Caregiving Experience

CAREGIVING AS AN INFORMAL SUPPORT

Family members and informal, non-public support systems provide most elder care (Cantor 1983; Montgomery, Gonyea and Hooyman 1985a). Informal social support is the largest component of long-term care in the U.S. (George 1986). Family, particularly adult children, not only provide more care in the form of services and emotional support than ever before but provide more difficult care over longer periods of time (Brody 1985b).

Multiple persons and systems provide care ranging from household maintenance to transportation to total care (Cantor 1980; Scott, Roberto and Hutton 1986). Caregiving tasks are grouped as: direct care (supervision and monitoring, performance of activities of daily living, advocacy and needs assessment); (intra)personal tasks and role adjustment (assumption of financial and emotional responsibility, resolve feelings about caregiving); and family ties, social/health care networks (manage family's practical and emotional issues and interface with formal systems to procure services and information) (Clark and Rakowski 1983). Horowitz (1985a) adds financial assistance, co-residence and caring for an institutionalized elder. Elder impairment and caregiver-elder relationship can predict amount and type of care (Horowitz 1985b; Noelker and Bass 1989; Stoller and Pugliesi 1989b). Specifically, caregivers of elders in poor health provide more hours of care (Stoller and Pugliesi 1989b, 326) and daughters tend to provide instrumental assistance (household help, meal preparation and/or personal care) than sons (Horowitz 1985b).

Family caregiving can impact those involved positively or negatively, particularly the primary caregiver. The positive effects of caregiving relate to the caregiver's ability to reciprocate for past care or fulfill a perceived familial obligation (Horowitz and Shindelman

7

1983). Caregivers generally report role satisfaction (O'Connor, Pollitt, Roth, Brook and Reiss 1990), with older caregivers more satisfied than younger caregivers (Worcester and Quayhagen 1983). Approximately eighty-three percent of the caregivers studied by Stoller and Pugliesi (1989a) felt their efforts improved the elders' quality of life. However, positive feelings often decrease as elders age (Worcester and Quayhagen 1983) and as problems increase. While the literature is generally conflicted on the effects of duration on caregiving, this finding suggests a relationship with duration of caregiving, decreasing health status and increasing care needs which may lead to increased strain.

Caregiving is a role (versus task) as the caregiver becomes embedded in the performance of the duties which are of extended duration and change in response to elder needs (Pearlin 1992). Tasks have a specified beginning and ending. The caregiver identifies him or herself with a role by tasks performed and commitment to future tasks. Individual identity becomes organized around the role (Karpel and Strauss 1983) which can have positive or negative effects depending on caregiver response to the role. If a caregiver thinks of caregiving as fulfilling a normal role, the caregiver can then assume an identity and behave consistently with the definition of caregiver. Defining caregiving as a role (versus task) may promote clarity of family and elder expectations of the caregiver.

Role designations result from family structure, history and competing commitments (Matthews and Rosner 1988). The caregiving role can be defined by elder needs, family resources and caregiver level of willingness to provide care. The role includes the provision of practical and emotional support to an elder no longer able to function independently due to physical or cognitive deterioration.

The Elderly as Care-Recipients

Caregiving needs are increasing due to rising elderly longevity. Americans live longer, healthier lives but have health problems requiring personal care (with activities of daily living) (Rowe and Kahn 1987). Life expectancy regardless of sex or race has been rising since 1900. In 1900, 4% of the population was considered elderly. By 1985, the number tripled (U.S. Select Committee on Aging 1987) and the definition of aging was changing. By 2000, this number may rise to 13% and by 2030, 22% of the American population is expected to be over 65 (Parsons and Cox 1989). During this same period of time, however, family members as caregiving resources for this growing population, have experienced significant changes. While the mean number of children born to a woman was 3.7 in 1900, this number has decreased to 1.8 in 1980 (National Center for Health Statistics 1987b).

Increases in average longevity range from 25 years (white males) to 40 years (African-American females) (National Center for Health Statistics 1987a). White males live an average 71.5 years, white females average 78.5 years, and persons of color live two to three years less (Crouch 1987; Older Women's League 1989). By 2005, males will live an average 74.1 years and females will live 81 years (Older Women's League 1989). Death rates for elderly have decreased 29% from 1950-1982 (Waldo and Lazenby 1984).

Needs increase with increased age, frailty and widowhood and decreased financial resources (Blieszner and Hamon, 1992). The "old-old" (85 years and older) present problems as they require higher levels of supportive care (Brody, Johnsen, Fulcomer and Lang 1983). The proportion of 65-79 year olds in institutions remained constant from 1950-1970, while those 80 years and older increased 50% during that period (Doty 1986). The old-old are requiring higher levels of care for a longer period of time than at any point in the past.

While most are functionally independent, approximately 23% of those 65 and older require assistance with activities of daily living (Doty 1986). Specifically, 20% of those 65-74 years old, 33% of those 75-84 years old and 55% of those over age 85 require assistance with at least one activity of daily living (Dawson, Hendershot and Fulton 1987). Nearly four-fifths live in their own or family homes (Doty 1986). For every institutionalized elder, two are cared for by family in the community (Shanas 1979a). Informal support systems are key to community living. Stone and colleagues (1987) describe the typical dependent elder as a married, 65-74 year old woman living with a spouse, low to middle income, in poor health who requires assistance with five to six activities of daily living.

Most elders have satisfying ongoing relationships with family members. Seventy percent share a household with family (Shanas 1979a and b). Most have at least one living sibling or child living nearby and have regular contacts with family. More than 75% see a child at least weekly and almost half daily (Shanas 1979a and b). The data reported approximately fourteen years ago has continued to hold true. Approximately two-thirds of elders live within thirty minutes of a child; 62% visit with children at least one time per week; and over three-fourths have weekly telephone contact (AARP/AOA 1992).

Most families maintain a certain amount of closeness and have frequent contacts, experiencing a phenomena referred to as "intimacy at a distance" (Moody 1994, 130). Elders report what they desire most from their family members is affection (Blieszner and Hamon 1992). In fact, individuals who perceived higher levels of social support reportedly experienced less depressive symptoms and better mental health overall (Wagoner and Bohannon 1995). While most elders prefer independence (Cicirelli 1981), more live and are sick longer due to improved technology; thus, family help is needed to retain independence. Most elders are females who live longer, provide most of the care, are widowed, poorer and more dependent on family and services than males. In the cases in which a female spouse is not available to provide care, the issue of who will provide the care is not as clear cut, but often falls to an adult child.

Adult Children as Caregivers

Family commitment to elder care enables approximately 95% of elders to remain in the community (AARP/AOA 1992). Yet, there is concern about family ability and willingness to respond to increasing needs (Stoller and Earl 1983). In fact, as Hagestad (1994) points out, societal norms may have created a philosophical trend which shifts the perceived responsibility of family care from the family to the individual, thus suggesting that caregiving of family members is a voluntary venture. Citing earlier work, Walker and Pratt (1991, 3) suggest ". . . there are no clear normative expectations regarding the behavior of adult children toward their aging parents." Empirical evidence is needed to validate current assumptions about family members' ability and willingness to provide care (Rathbone-McCuan, Hooyman and Fortune 1985).

Cox (1993) and Brittain and Dellmann-Jenkins (1995) examined the perceived filial expectations of adult children regarding their obligation to provide care to elderly parents. The findings of this research suggest that there is a strong adherence to filial support. Specifically, 85% of African-American respondents and 73% of White respondents reported a perceived obligation to provide care (Cox 1993), leading Cox to posit that "cultural values may influence the experience of these caregivers" (1993, 39). This further supports the recommendation by Rathborn-McCuan and colleagues (1985) regarding the need for further research in this area. Brittain and Dellman-Jenkins (1995) found younger adults (age 18–40 years) to also possess high levels of filial responsibility which does not decrease when the individual is engaged in caregiving.

Elder care has traditionally been provided by female family members (Anastas, Gibeau and Larson 1990; Braithwaite 1986; Goldstein, Regnery and Willin 1981; Jones and Vetter 1984; Reece, Walz and Hageboeck 1983; Stone, et al. 1987). Stone and colleagues (1987) report 72% of caregivers are female (primarily daughters and wives), with most male caregivers being spouses. Spouse caregivers provide the most extensive care (Johnson 1983) and are more tolerant of impairments (Crossman, London and Barry 1981). Many report being sole, primary caregivers (approximately 33% in the Informal Caregivers Survey, Stone, et al. 1987) who receive formal and informal assistance with caregiving (39% in Stone, et al. 1987). Females provide sole care more than males.

When a spouse is unavailable, daughters usually serve as primary caregivers. A hierarchical model based on caregiver's kinship relationship to the elder supports gender-ordered role assumption (daughter, daughter-in-law, son, younger female relative, younger male relative and non-relative) (Soldo and Myllyuoma 1983). Recent research has supported this traditional conceptualization of caregiving. Elders' preferences for care include, in order: 1) immediate family members; 2) other family members; and 3) paid help (Draughn, Tiller, McKellar and Dunaway 1995).

Regardless of the sibling network, higher proportions of daughters provide more care than sons; males with no siblings are an exception (Coward and Dwyer 1990). Same sex children are more likely to provide care (Stoller 1990), which explains the higher numbers of daughter caregivers.

Not only do females provide more care, they provide care earlier, longer and perform more personal care tasks, while males (except spouses) provide advisory, financial and household maintenance help (Horowitz 1985b; Houser, Berkman and Bardsley 1988; Stoller 1990; Young and Kahana 1989). Stoller (1990) reports a weak but significant relationship between male withdrawal and increased care needs.

Rooted in traditional gender role expectations, evidence suggests gender is key to induction. Gender is an important and consistent predictor of caregiver involvement (Horowitz 1985b). Females are the preferred caregivers. Daughters are twice as likely to stay near parents (Ikels 1983) and being female predicts stronger filial obligation (Finley, Roberts and Banahan 1988) and willingness and ability to provide care (Kivett and Atkinson 1984).

Stone and colleagues (1987) describe the typical caregiver as 57.3 years old with daughter caregivers being 45–64 years old, in low to middle income brackets, married, in good health and living with the elder. Sons and other relatives are usually secondary caregivers (Cantor 1980; Horowitz 1985b; Stone, et al. 1987). Length of care ranges from weeks to decades, with an average being one to four years (Stone, et al. 1987).

With the number of elders increasing, parent care may be inevitable. Forty percent of 50 year olds, 30% of 60 year olds and 3% of 70 year olds have a living parent (Brody 1985b). Couples are likely to have more parents than children (U.S. Select Committee on Aging 1987). Social factors affecting family willingness and ability to provide high level care include: decreased fertility, high divorce rate, low remarriage rate, and increased women's labor force participation (Crouch 1987; Pratt and Kethley 1988). Delayed child bearing may result in providing care to parents while minor children are at home (one-fourth to one-third in the Informal Caregivers Survey) (Stone et al. 1987).

As the number of elderly increases, fewer younger relatives are available to provide care (Hooyman and Ryan 1987). Increasing divorce rates and declining remarriages result in fewer available caregivers and money (Pratt and Kethley 1988). Evidence is conflicted regarding care responsibilities of single adult children. Single family members are reported to have both more and less responsibility than married members (Cicirelli 1984; Ikels 1983; and Stoller 1983).

Single members can be less able or willing to provide care due to daily pressures or family relationship problems (Cicirelli 1984). Type of marital disruption does not affect type or amount of care provided. High divorce and low remarriage rates may increase burden, reducing ability to invest time and financial resources into care. Increases in the numbers of non-traditional families (homosexual families, unmarried and childless couples) and working women limit available support persons, as these families have fewer members to provide care and as women enter and stay in the labor force (Pratt and Kethley 1988).

CAREGIVER STRAIN

Issues of Measurement

A number of definitions of caregiver strain (stress) have been introduced in the literature in the past two decades. An early definition of caregiver stress/strain was developed by Fatherington, Skelton and Hoddinott (1972) which conceptualized "burden" as "specific changes in caregivers' day-to-day lives such as disruption of daily routine" (in Poulshock and Deimling 1984). Pearlin and Schooler (1978, 3) later defined caregiving "strain" as "enduring problems that have the potential for arousing threat, a meaning that establishes strain and stressor as interchangeable concepts." In 1980, Zarit, Reever and Bach-Peterson defined "burden" as the caregiver's perception of such problem behaviors as: caregiver health; psychological well-being; finances; social life; and the relationship between the caregiver and the elder. Poulshock and Deimling (1984, 230) later specified "burden" as "a mediating force between elders' impairments and impact on caregivers." This suggests that burden is the subjective caregiver perception of caregiving which results in the objective impact of the experience. Robinson (1983) adopts Pearlin and Schooler's perspective of caregiving strain as an objective experience that has the potential for arousing threat; she developed a caregiver strain inventory to measure the presence of caregiver strain.

Despite widespread use of the concepts of stress, burden and strain, clarity and operational definitions and methods to quantify the concept are lacking (Given, Collins and Given 1988; Poulshock and Deimling 1984). Attempts to quantify strain and stress by measuring elder characteristics and subjective and objective perceptions of stress have been made, but there are questions regarding concepts actually measured by "stress or burden" scales (Gallo 1990; George and Gwyther 1986; Novak and Guest 1989a). Despite frequent use, strain and stress scales may not accurately measure types and depth of caregiver strain or strain with a relational or cultural context. Further, caregiver motivations to provide care are not typically included in a measure of caregiver strain (Walker, et al. 1995). A number of scales have been developed to measure strain, stress and burden; eleven are reviewed here (see Appendix A). Five scale development efforts used samples of caregivers of demented elders; six used caregivers of physically ill elders or mixed samples. Samples sizes range from 29 to 614 (8<100). All scales are summative, producing a score measuring level of strain or stress. With the exception of the Burden Inventory (Zarit, Reever and Bach-Peterson 1980), most of the scales have limited use and findings may be an artifact of caregiver stress/strain scales being in the early stages of development. While multi-dimensional measures capture varied aspects of caregiving, these scales include global items which both limit reliability and fail to differentiate between categories.   While all the strain and stress measures reviewed report adequate reliability and validity levels, these measures are criticized for their inability to distinguish between dimensions of burden because they produce a single summary score (Novak and Guest 1989a). The lack of a specific definition of strain/stress results in an inability to develop a precise measure (Poulshock and Deimling 1984).

The terms caregiver "strain", "stress" and "burden" are used interchangeably throughout the literature. Since this discussion is an aggregation of the strain and stress literature, the term "strain" will be used here. Other terms will be used only if it is appropriate to use the cited author(s)' words.

Factors Related to Caregiver Strain

It is important to understand how this research will add to our knowledge of caregiver strain. After presenting an overview of the problems of caregiving, elder, caregiver, relationship and caregiving arrangement characteristics in identifying factors related to strain will be discussed. Appendix B presents empirical findings related to strain.

Problems cited by caregivers include: fatigue, anger, depression, family conflict, emotional strain, missing the elder as he/she had been and concern for caregiver illness (Barusch 1988; Cantor 1983; George and Gwyther 1986; Rabins, Mace and Lucas 1982). Stress and inadequate coping skills serve to mediate psychiatric symptoms (depression and anxiety estimates are up to 50%) (Toseland and Rossiter 1989). In a three-year study of caregivers of demented elders, 20% were found to experience syndromal depression and 33% experienced episodic depression, while 47% reported no depressive experiences (Redinbaugh, MacCallum and Kiecolt-Glaser 1995). Caregiving can result in: guilt, self-blame, psychosomatic disorders, family conflict and interpersonal problems (Toseland and Rossiter 1989). Additional negative results include concern for the elder, time constraints and employment, health and interpersonal relationship problems (Horowitz 1985a) and problems with household performance, social activities and marital satisfaction (Hoyert and Seltzer 1992). The demands can cause sleep loss, health problems, shattered social lives and feelings of isolation.

Moderate to extreme levels of stress are reported (80+% in Johnson, 1983 and 89–93% in Steinmetz 1988), but, given high care demand, negative outcomes are less than expected (Horowitz 1985a). Factors related to stress include: personality and behavior change, family history, coping ability, available social support, expectation versus perception of support received, competing demands and caregiver and elder characteristics (Ory, et al. 1985). Hoyert and Seltzer (1992) additionally cite duration of caregiving as a potential factor creating stress accumulation. Information in the literature conflicts regarding caregiver strain outcomes and their causes, but the evidence suggests the experience of caregiving can produce strain.

Elder Factors. Studies suggest that caregiver strain may be influenced by such elder factors as cognitive and physical health impairment. Worcester and Quayhagen (1983) report elders with psychological problems provide caregivers with a more difficult task of caregiving than elders with physical health problems. Caregivers of elders with cognitive impairments relate stress to the number of memory and behavioral problems and elder personality change (Barusch and Spaid 1989; Biegel, Sales and Schulz 1991; Rabins et al. 1982). Elder illness factors are associated with increased caregiver strain. The elder's social withdrawal, inappropriate behavior and physical limitations associated with dementia are major contributors of caregiver stressors (hassles) (Kinney and Stephens 1989b). Kinney and Stephens (1989b, 328) define caregiving hassles as "transient and chronic events that are appraised by an individual as threatening his or her well-being." Elder social withdrawal accounts for 22.4% and the elder's inappropriate behaviors explains 23% of the variance in behavioral stressors (hassles), while degree of elder physical limitations account for 17.1% of the in variance of ADL stressors (hassles). Novak and Guest (1989) report functional decline of demented elders explains 14% of the variance in caregiver stress. A positive correlation exists between elder activities of daily living (ADL) (r = .26) and instrumental activities of daily living (IADL) (r = .28) limitations (Pearson, Verma and Nellett 1988). Poulshock and Deimling (1984, 234) report a "moderate-to-strong" relationship between elder impairment and perceived caregiver burden. Using a linear probability sample of elders and their caregivers, Stoller and Pugliesi (1989b) report health and functional status negatively impact the caregiver. Characteristics of the elder's physical illness are related to the caregiver's perceived load (Oberst, Thomas, Gass and Ward 1989). While these findings suggest elders in poor health require more care which can create higher levels of burden, they do not explain the relationship between dementing illness, physical decline and the caregiver's perception of the caregiving responsibility (which may be more related to his/her perception of the elder's cognitive/personality change than to the physical changes).

Phase of illness and duration of caregiving may affect response, but the findings are conflicted. Strain and stress have been reported to be highest in both the early phase (Chenoweth and Spencer 1986;

Novak and Guest 1989) and middle phase of an illness, particularly a dementing illness (Chiriboga, Weiler and Nielsen 1988–89), and it is reported to decrease in the later phase (Zarit, Todd and Zarit 1986). Yet, duration of caregiving can negatively impact the caregiver's experience. As elder needs increase over time, caregiver stress increases (Oberst, et al. 1989). Years of caregiving is related to increased psychological distress, particularly for caregivers with little social support (Baille, et al. 1988). These conflicting findings may indicate that other factors impact strain but have been captured only in terms of issues related to time of illness and caregiving.

Caregiver Factors. Gender, age, relationship to elder, attitude toward caregiving and health influence strain. Studies show women experience more strain than men (Anthony-Bergstone, Zarit and Gatz 1988; Biegel, et al. 1991; O'Connor, et al. 1990; Young and Kahana 1989) since they provide more care earlier, longer, and with higher demands placed upon them (Biegel, et al. 1991). Females report higher levels of strain, which may be due to women caring for older, sicker elders (Barusch and Spaid 1989), guilt related to traditional gender role expectations (Brody, Hoffman, Kleban and Schoonover 1989); and less help and support, intimacy and affection from elders and other family members (Creasy, Myers, Epperson and Taylor 1990). Females alter schedules more often than males, and elders more often expect them to do so (Stone, et al. 1987).

The caregiving role is more often prescribed for women than men which results in a lack of perceived options for women. Women use less formal and informal help (Baillie, Norbeck and Barnes 1988; Morycz 1985; Sauer and Coward 1985) and report they do not cope as well as men with the responsibility of caregiving (Barusch and Spaid 1989), which may be an artifact of self-report measures. The more care provided, particularly personal care, the more stress the caregiver perceives (Oberst, et al. 1989; Stoller and Pugliesi 1989a). In a meta-analysis of gender differences in caregiving, Miller and Cafasso (1992) report gender explains only 4% of the variance in burden, but female caregivers are 20% more burdened than male counterparts. This may be explained by the fact that women perform more personal care and household tasks. Further study is needed as the effect is small and practical significance is in question.

Younger caregivers also report more stress (Stephens, Norris, Kinney, Ritchie and Grotz 1988) and an increased sense of self-loss (engulfment in the caregiving role) due to competing responsibilities (Skaff and Pearlin 1992). They are probably married children (daughters) with competing demands (Horowitz 1985b; Johnson, 1983; Jones and Vetter, 1984). However, married daughters report more positive experiences with caregiving as increased amounts of support and income are available to them in performing caregiving tasks (Brody, Litvin, Hoffman and Kleban 1992). Caregiver age may also be related to the caregiver's relationship to the elder, which itself is associated with strain and stress. Adult children report more stress than other caregivers (O'Connor, et al. 1990; Young and Kahana 1989) due to competing role obligations. Competing roles promote stress when care demands are high (Stoller and Pugliesi 1989a). An examination of such caregiver factors as age, marital status and competing roles may provide greater understanding of the contribution of each of these factors to caregiver strain.

Caregiver attitude can predict future strain. When controlling for the elder's functional level, the caregivers' subjective assessments of the "all-encompassing nature of providing care," particularly the perception of the time demands and high global stress, contributes more to social limitations than objective activities (Miller and Montgomery 1990). Caregivers who perceive a lack of available support report more stress (Fiore, Becker and Coppel 1983). Stress is also attributed to caregiver perception of family support as measured by the number of visits to the elder/caregiver made by family members (Zarit, Reever and Bach-Peterson 1980). These findings suggest the importance of measuring the caregiver's perception of multiple facets of the caregiving experience, which has not been conducted to date.

Caregiver perception of the elder and the relationship have been linked to caregiver strain. Caregivers who perceive the elder as more severely ill report higher stress (Biegel, et al. 1991), as do those who view elder cognitive status as poor (Pratt, Schmall and Wright 1986). These findings concur with previously cited studies, which suggests elder illness impacts caregiver strain and stress. They may then suggest that subjective caregiver perception of elder's health is related to objective elder physical and mental health status.

Additional relationships are suggested between caregiver strain and perception of the caregiving situation. Stress levels are higher for caregivers who report not feeling emotionally close to the elder prior to assuming the caregiving role (Pratt, et al. 1986). Caregivers who perceive limited resources, increased demands on their time and energy and increased impact also experience higher levels of stress (Montgomery 1992). Limited future outlook related to the caregiving relationship may increase caregiver stress levels (Rakowski and Clark 1985). Caregivers who report poorer health experience more stress (Biegel, et al. 1991; Pratt, et al. 1986).

Race and culture seem to impact caregiver response to caregiving. Preliminary data reported by Haley, Collins, Wadley, Harrell and Roth (1992) and Lawton, Rajagopal, Brody and Kleban (1992) suggests African-American caregivers are less stressed and more self-efficacious than white caregivers. Further, African-Americans are more stressed by elder factors (functional level), while white caregivers are more stressed by elder living arrangement (alone) and lack of social support (Morycz, Malloy and Martz 1987). African-American families, relative to white families, may be better prepared for caregiving due to the tradition of the extended family network (Taylor and Chatters 1989).

Research shows that while controlling for socioeconomic status, African-American daughter caregivers report lower levels of role strain (88%) than white daughters (91%) (Mui 1992). Predictors of strain/stress for African-American caregivers include: poor health, lack of respite support, role demands and life conflict. White daughter caregivers' stress is associated with: poor mother-daughter relationships (weaker familial obligation) and work conflict (due to a shorter history of working than African-American women).

African-American daughters are thought to have a stronger sense of filial obligation than White daughters; thus, they will feel obligated to provide care to parents regardless of the quality or history of their current or previous relationship with the parent. Additionally, African-American daughters reported higher levels of satisfaction and mastery with the caregiving role and less feelings of intrusion into their lives as a result of the caregiving responsibilities (Lawton, et al. 1992). These findings suggest caregiver strain may be associated with factors related to the family's ethnicity and cultural influences. Additional study is needed to shed light on the impact of these factors on caregiver induction into the caregiving role. However, sociodemographic and cultural issues should be addressed when considering racial differences in caregiving (Haley, et al. 1992).

In recent years, the concept of familial and societal culture as a predictor of the caregiving experience, has consistently emerged in the caregiving literature. Choi (1993), for example, suggests two cultural factors, caregiver congruency with cultural norms regarding caregiving and acceptance of cultural norms regarding caregiving, are noted as predictors of caregiver burden. The evidence noted in this review serves to support the premise that cultural expectations and norms should be included in caregiving research.

Relationship Factors. Studies examining the impact of the caregiver-elder relationship on strain or stress suggest caregiver strain/stress can be a result of: 1) poor caregiver-elder relationship (Scharlach, 1987) or lack of caregiver affection for the elder (Mancini and Blieszner 1989); 2) a high level of perceived caregiver-elder closeness (Kahana and Young 1991); and 3) caregiver social and emotional losses and sacrifices which result from assuming the caregiving role (Doty 1986). Caregiver role strain can occur when individual caregivers feel the larger family unit should be responsible for care, but care is provided by only the caregiver and not multiple members of the family (Cantor 1983).

While feelings of caregiver attachment for the elder have been found to predict caregiving behavior and result in decreased subjective burden, feelings of filial obligation have been shown to result in increased self-monitoring to ensure performance of caregiving tasks (versus responding to parental needs) and are linked to increased subjective burden (Cicirelli 1993). Perhaps, then relationship history and attitude toward caregiving may impact caregiver motivation and sense of obligation to provide care. These factors may influence perceived strain as the caregiver with a history of conflict with the elder may not feel obligated to provide care.

Caregiving Arrangement Factors. While co-residing with the elder results in increased helping, co-residence has also been shown to create increased stress for the caregiver (Biegel, et al. 1991; Eagles, et al. 1987; Hoyert and Seltzer 1992; Reece, et al. 1983) and dependence by the care-recipient (Cicirelli 1993), as the tasks are more intense, constant and strenuous. Others suggest co-residence is not stressful (Pearson, et al. 1988; Staight and Harvey 1990; Stoller and Pugliesi 1989a), as it enables the caregiver to limit other role responsibilities and focus his/her attention primarily on caregiving. These inconsistencies may be resolved by controlling for other factors when examining the relationship between residence and caregiver strain. Essentially, however, little is known about the motivations for intergenerational co-residence and the exchange relationships which precede or occur related to co-residence (Ward and Spitz 1992).

Stress results when the caregiving tasks are viewed by the caregiver as confining (Robinson and Thurnher 1979). Care-related tasks that confine the caregiver (identified as objective burden [constant supervision and performing activities of daily living]) are more stressful as they restrict activities (Montgomery, et al. 1985b). This finding may vary according to how caregivers define "confining," which may be related to the caregiver's perception of how or why he/she assumed the role.

In sum, female, daughter and co-resident caregivers provide more care longer to sicker elders and consistently report higher levels of stress/strain. Chronic caregiving problems can lead to stress in one area (health, for example) and cause deterioration in other areas (relationships) (Chiriboga, et al. 1988–89). Stress can be positive if it promotes family cohesion and solidarity (Masciocchi, et al. 1984). Caregivers can adapt, drawing on existing resources or developing new strategies (Stephens and Zarit 1989). Yet stress also has negative consequences. It is linked to premature institutionalization (Colerick and George 1986; Ory, et al. 1985) and elder abuse and neglect (Douglass 1983; Giordano and Giordano 1984; Kosberg 1988) and may be a stronger predictor of abuse than amount or duration of care (Steinmetz 1988).

INDUCTION TO CAREGIVING

Knowledge about role induction in general can provide insight into caregiver role induction. Orlinsky and Howard (1978) suggest induction into therapy is an evolving process involving normative organization of roles and experiences. Caregiving roles also evolve with the changing needs of a situation but may be based on family experiences and abilities (history of caregiving in the family and available psychological and practical resources to provide care). Caregiving roles and tasks occur within the organizational context of the family unit and can change as perceived needs and resources change.

In clinical therapy, interventions in role induction are aimed at improving retention and outcome through clarifying role expectations; and it has been shown to be an effective tool in achieving these goals. This therapeutic relationship is a consensus of intentions, influenced by the power possessed by each participant which serves to meet "mutual if not equal interests" (Orlinsky and Howard 1978, 308). While a therapeutic relationship has distinct limits and boundaries, the definition of caregiving is often unclear due to the previous relationship history. Despite history, lack of clarity regarding boundaries and expectations may frustrate the caregiver and potentially lead to negative outcomes.

The literature suggests two factors, caregiver characteristics and caregiving resources, may relate to role induction. These factors determine who is selected, how and when the process occurs, why the caregiver is selected and tasks to be performed. Ikels (1983) suggests caregiver induction influences the outcome of caregiving. For example, children who alter marriage, employment or relocation opportunities to provide care may react negatively to the elder and caregiving.

While care is usually provided by a spouse when available, spouses are becoming increasingly unavailable due to death, divorce or disability. In the absence of a spouse, adult children often provide care, choosing the quantity and type of care they wish to provide (Cantor 1980). While research often focuses on spouse or caregiver-elder dyads, in reality several adult children can be involved (Matthews and Rosner 1988). Due to the ambiguities of social rules dictating elder care, children can determine caregiver identity and level of involvement. Less is known about how adult child caregivers come to assume and carry out the role. For these reasons, this investigation focuses on intergenerational caregiving between elders and their adult children.

The caregiving role can be considered a consensual contract between parties with a relationship history involving distinct levels of power (parent-child relationship). This arrangement meets both elder (to receive help) and caregiver needs (to provide help and know the elder is receiving help). Caregiving induction can be unique due to situation characteristics, but events associated with induction into caregiving can include, but are not limited to: 1) identification of caregiving need; 2) selection of caregiver; 3) designation of level of involvement (primary, secondary or peripheral); 4) identification and mobilization of individual/family resources to provide care (economic, living arrangements, health/social care, etc.); 5) designation of tasks to be performed; and 6) implementation of arrangement. This process occurs in response to elder need for care. The onset of the caregiving may be gradual and expected or sudden and unexpected. Timing influences both role assumption and adjustment.

Little is known from the empirical literature about who is selected to provide care to elderly family members, how and why the selection is made and the impact of selection on the caregiver. However, discussions are found in four areas of the literature which relate to the way in which caregivers come to assume the role. These areas are: 1) caregiver identity; 2) reasons caregivers are selected for the role; 3) proximity or living arrangement; and 4) willingness to assume the role.

1) *Caregiver Identity.* Related factors can be grouped as: a) gender, b) relationship to elder, c) marital status and d) socioeconomic or employment status.

a) *Gender.* Despite society's expressed attitudes regarding equitable distribution of care, women continue to provide the majority of care (Brody 1985a, 179). Eighty to ninety percent of adult child caregivers are female (Stone, et al. 1987). Daughters provide more care than sons (Coward and Dwyer 1990; Coward, Horne and Dwyer

1992; Horowitz 1985b; Houser, et al. 1985) regardless of the sibling network (Coward and Dwyer 1990). Women serve as primary caregivers due to a continued acceptance of traditional gender-appropriate roles in society (George 1986, 80, citing Cantor 1979; Mui 1990, 13). Thirty-four percent of community-dwelling elders receive care from their daughters (Coward, et al. 1992). As previously noted, female caregivers view caregiving more negatively, which may be a result of the perceived responsibility of being forced to provide care.

b) Relationship to Elder. Most non-spouse primary caregivers are daughters who provide more direct or personal care, while sons and other relatives serve as secondary caregivers who provide occasional/indirect care (Stone, et al. 1987). In fact, daughters most often provide care to elderly mothers (41%) (Coward, et al. 1992). Daughters in all sibling groups provide more care than sons (Coward and Dwyer, 1990). Sons assume more responsibility during stages of family life when dependent children are in the home but transfer responsibility to a spouse later in life (Stoller 1983). Additionally, as elders age, daughters' rates of caregiving also increase: 36.4% for 65–74 year old elders; 47.4% for 75–84 year old elders; and 51.6% for elders 85 years and older (Coward, et al. 1992).

Montgomery (1992) offers four explanation for increased adult daughter care (versus son): 1) perceived time available—despite increased participation in the labor market, women continue to be viewed as have time for family members; 2) external resources—may be related to the division of family labor, familial power and financial resources available to women; 3) socialization or ideology—relates to the ways in which filial obligations are fulfilled (specifically, task specializations); and 4) specification of tasks—relates to the tradition that males perform "male" tasks (financial, household maintenance, etc.) and females perform *all* tasks.

Daughters are highly influential in parental (particularly mothers) decision-making on health, finances and housing due to knowledge of preferences and health status (Pratt, Jones, Shin and Walker 1989). Understanding that families prefer daughter caregivers adds insight into reports of higher levels of daughter caregiver strain, which may result from higher levels of care provision.

Of non-child caregivers, daughters-in-law are more involved than sons-in-law (Horowitz 1985b), supporting the idea that traditional gender role expectations override relationship. Empirical support is lacking for other relatives as numbers and roles are smaller and more peripheral.

c) *Marital Status.* The literature is conflicted regarding the relationship between marital status and caregiving role induction. Single children are reported to provide more care (Ikels 1983; Stoller 1983; Shellenberger, et al. 1989). Single children perceive they provide equal amounts of care as married siblings, while married children perceive single siblings provide less care (Cicirelli 1984). Gaps exist in our knowledge base regarding the role of marital status on caregiving induction and strain. Examining this area may further our understanding of the impact of family of origin relationships on later life events.

d) *Socioeconomic Status (SES).* Caregiver socioeconomic status can determine level of involvement (identity) (Stoller 1983). Employed children provide fewer hours of care, but not less care (Lang and Brody 1983). Caregivers with higher educational levels who are employed more hours outside the home provide less emotional support (Houser, et al. 1985). Children with higher socioeconomic status levels purchase care, while those with lower socioeconomic status levels perform more care tasks themselves (Archbold 1983; Cicirelli 1981). Mitchell and Register (1984) find persons with fewer resources are more likely to share more of their available resources than those with greater resources. Interestingly, a higher caregiver socioeconomic status level has been shown to result in lower feelings of attachment for the elder (Cicirelli 1993). While caregiver socioeconomic status may be related to the choice of a caregiver and the implementation of the caregiving plan, the relationship between socioeconomic status and the impact of caregiving for the caregiver is not clear.

2) Reasons For Selection. Caregiver responses to inquiries regarding why caregivers care suggest the decision-making process is often complex and involves numerous factors. Reasons for selection may be, in fact, a combination of the caregiver's sense of filial obligation *and* the affection felt by the caregiver toward the elder

(Montgomery 1992). Caregivers cite reasons they are selected which range from situational to emotional. However, ". . . motives that prompt adult children to care for their frail parents are not well understood. . ." (Montgomery 1992, 67). While study is beginning to examine who is selected to provide care and the reasons caregivers are selected for caregiving, there has been no exploration into the relationship between these factors and an outcome of caregiving, such as strain.

Using content analysis of in-depth interviews, Guberman and colleagues (1992) report six primary and eight secondary categories determine selection. The primary categories include: 1) love and feelings of family ties; 2) inadequacy of institutional/community resources; 3) profound need to help others; 4) feelings of duty and obligation; 5) imposition of the decision by the dependent person; and 6) women's socioeconomic status dependence (caregiver assumes role in order to have access to elder's economic resources). Secondary determinants are: 1) unavailability of other family members; 2) anti-institution feelings; 3) caregiving arrangement (availability of support); 4) religious feelings; 5) caregiver's personal characteristics (availability); 6) belief in the healing process; 7) dependent person's health status; and 8) family tradition. These categories are grouped into three clusters: 1) factors related to the caregiver's material, social and psychological status—love, need to help, duty, socioeconomic dependence, anti-institutional feelings, caregiving arrangement, religious feelings, personal characteristics, belief in healing and family tradition; 2) factors related to availability of resources— inadequate or unavailable family, community and institutional resources; and 3) factors related to the care-receiver—imposition and health. While caregiver factors are the strongest determinants, Guberman and colleagues (1992, 615) report interconnectedness between factors, suggesting "any attempt to explain the process must take into account the complexity of main and secondary factors, precipitating and incidental factors that come into play, interact and are transformed over time ."

Albert (1990) cites three reasons for caregiver role assumption: 1) repayment of a debt; 2) no one else will do it; and 3) no one else should do it. Further, Albert (1190, 322–323) identifies four reasons for selection: 1) caregiving is a return to one's parents; 2) caregiving is caring for part of one's self; 3) the impaired parent is viewed as an ill person; and 4) the impaired parent is viewed as a child. Caregivers who perceive caregiving as an exchange process view the parent as ill, while those who feel filially obligated (view parent as part of one's self) perceive the parent as a child. Parent-child conflict is associated with caregiver reasons for caregiving. The adult child becomes frustrated with the lack of intimacy which results from a poor parent-child relationship and feels conflicted regarding his/her views of the parent's needs.

Lawton and colleagues (1992) present a framework for identifying caregiver selection into the role. This framework measures the caregivers's traditional caregiver ideology through the use of a four–item index of caregiver attitude toward caregiving: 1) "wish to repay the debt of being cared for as a child"; 2) "continuing a family tradition of mutual concern"; 3) "fulfilling personal values"; and 4) "setting an example for one's children" (Lawton, et al. 1992, S159). Findings from research using this framework suggests that those caregivers who subscribe to a traditional caregiving ideology experience less caregiving-related burden, higher satisfaction with the role and, generally, report a more positive caregiving experience overall.

Cicirelli (1993, 144) suggests children essentially want to remain close to their parents and posits that through "early socialization to norms of expected filial behavior, adult children come to feel it is their duty, obligation or responsibility to help their elderly parents." Filial obligation, within this framework, is defined as an adherence to an internalized standard of proper filial behavior based on the cultural standards of that family. Motivators for parental caregiving based on Cicirelli's (1993) work include: filial obligation, attachment and protective behavior and attachment and obligation are linked to the amount of care that adult children actually provide to the elderly parent.

An additional framework is for caregiver selection into the role is presented by Blieszner and Hamon (1992). This conceptualization suggests that filial responsibility for care is determined by two caregiver factors: 1) appropriate behavior and responsibility on the part of the caregiver and 2) prevention of elder dependence. These factors are viewed as being related to the adult child's expectations regarding the caregiving role. Specifically, adult children's perceptions regarding filial obligation are derived from such life satisfaction factors as costs and rewards of the relationship, geographic proximity and competing roles.

The concept of altruism as a motivation for caregiving is yet another perspective from which caregiver reason for selection into the caregiving role may be viewed. Altruism may be defined as the ". . . interpersonal orientation or motivation underlying helping behavior in general and caregiving, in particular" (Midlarsky, 1994). As opposed to reciprocity in which an exchange of services is expected, altruism is based on the expectation that no extrinsic reward will be received by the provider of the service. The service or task is performed out of a "desire to benefit another, whatever the cost of oneself" (Midlarsky, 1994, 91). Despite the lack of tangible expected gains, the result of helping for the caregiver may be experienced in the form of: 1) distraction from other concerns or loneliness; 2) attaining value congruence; 3) increased sense of control or competence; and/or 4) satisfaction (Midlarsky, 1994, 88). Inherent within this framework is the notion that caregivers whose motivations for caregiving are altruistic in nature will enjoy a more positive caregiving experience.

3) Proximity and Living Arrangement. Caregiver proximity to the elder has been measured as distance (time or miles) caregiver resides from the elder or household composition if caregiver and elder co-reside. Proximity has been associated with role induction. Specifically, most elders prefer not to live with non-spouse family members (Blieszner and Mancini 1987). Elders and families agree close proximity/co-residence is not needed to provide care (Hamon 1988; Hamon and Blieszner 1990; Hanson, Sauer and Seelbach 1983). Regarding the reason for caregiver induction, residential proximity is related to sense of familial obligation (Finley, et al. 1988) as distance results in decreased obligation to help or a decreased sense of obligation enables increased residential distance. Proximity is associated with willingness and ability to provide care (Kivett and Anderson 1984).

Living arrangement has been associated with identifying the caregiver and understanding why he/she is selected. One-third of roles are assumed for reasons related to caregiver-elder proximity (Older Women's League 1989). Daughters live closer to parents than sons

(Horowitz, 1985b), and women are more likely to live with daughters than sons when care is needed (Horowitz 1985b; Lang and Brody 1983), suggesting a proximate daughter is a likely caregiver. Regarding motivation for caregiving as it relates to co-residence, elders more often live with daughters for reasons related to companionship (Ward and Spitze 1992).

Penning (1990) reports that proximity (with caregiver group size, resources and nature of commitment) predicts tasks which the caregiver will perform. Ikels (1983), however, reports identity and role assumption is based on the most proximate child's location (when need occurs), and gender and is culturally determined.

Proximity (with availability) is a better predictor of caregiving role assumption than gender or birth order differences (Houser, et al. 1985; Tennstedt, Crawford and McKinlay 1993). Proximate, unemployed children provide more care than proximate employed siblings (Matthews, Wekner and Delaney 1989). While close proximity does not guarantee care, elders report children who reside fifty or more miles away help less than closer siblings (Montgomery and Hirshorn 1991).

Proximity increases opportunity to provide care (Lee 1980) and is related to familial obligation (Finley et al., 1988) which can determine helping behavior (Cicirelli 1981). Proximate caregivers can respond quickly and provide care longer with less disruption than those less proximate.

4) Willingness to Assume the Role. While seldom discussed in the literature (George 1986; Mancini and Blieszner 1989), willingness to assume the caregiving role can be linked to caregiver strain. Due to a lack of standardized measures which adequately capture the subjective meaning given to the caregiving experience by people, willingness is difficult to define, as it involves subjective evaluation of the situation and ambiguity of role definition (George 1986). Willingness is defined here as an acceptance by choice with little or no reluctance.

All things being equal, awareness and acceptance of family "rules" regarding caregiving (defined by culture, ethnicity, development or structure) can result in a caregiver more willing to assume the role. In a related study, Berg-Weger and Rubio (1996), caregivers who perceived no other viable alterantives to providing care also report decreased levels of willingness to serve as the primary caregiver. Caregiver ability to provide care, number of candidates and amount of resources are factors associated with level of willingness (Mancini and Blieszner 1989). Pre-caregiving feelings and the relationship can determine caregiver volunteering or being forced into the role (Given, et al. 1988). Initial willingness to provide care can erode as care needs increase and supports decrease. Eggert, Granger, Morris and Pendleton (1977) report a decrease from 70% to 38% in family willingness to provide care between a first and second hospital discharge. Lack of willingness (caregiving based on obligation alone) can lead to decreased quality of care provided (George 1986).

Willingness has been linked to experience of the elder's hospitalization. Specifically, longer hospital stays result in increased caregiver willingness to assume the role (Cox and Verdieck 1994). This increased willingness may provide the caregiver with an opportunity to prepare for the caregiving role by resolving other competing demands and/or mobilize resources. The caregiving experience prior to the hospitalization also impacted the caregiver's willingness to provide care as well. Those caregivers who had been less involved with the elder were more likely to institutionalize the elder, while those with higher levels of involvement prior to the hospitalization or strong feelings of filial obligation were more often undecided in their feelings toward nursing home placement, suggesting a willingness to provide non-institutionalized care (Cox and Verdieck 1994). The latter finding may be a residual effect of the caregiver's perceived lack of support leading to caregiver burnout). A similar finding by Pearlman and Crown (1992) suggests that those elders with a long-term (at least three years) caregiving relationship with a family member were less likely to be institutionalized than those with short-term relationships or recipients of services provided by formal (paid) supports.

Willingness to provide care may further be decreased due to: increased geographic family mobility and divorce and remarriage rates, decreased family size and changing sex roles (Ory, et al. 1985). Elders may not always assume that family members will be available or willing to provide care or that those who provide care are willingly doing so (Aldous 1994). Caregiver role assumption may be a result of unwillingness of other family members—one in four caregivers assume the role due to the unwillingness of others (Older Women's League 1989). Further, elders, family members and policy makers should not assume that caregivers' levels of willingness and ability to provide care will be sustained indefinitely (Aldous 1994). As noted, caregivers may provide care, in some form, for several decades and may be unable or unwilling to do so at the same or increasing levels.

In sum, the literature regarding caregivers' reasons for assuming the caregiving role is growing. This literature encompasses both the tangible and intangible aspects of the role. However, much remains to be learned regarding this phenomena. While the research and literature suggest that such factors as closeness of the relationship (child versus other relative), gender (female versus male) and physical proximity to the elder influence selection, this review has highlighted numerous other factors that impact the caregiver's motivation and ability to initiate and provide care.

THEORETICAL PERSPECTIVES

Empirical work on caregiving has often been atheoretical. Because no theory specifically addresses caregiver role induction, it is necessary to draw on theories used to explain broader aspects of caregiving. Two theories support the relationship between caregiver induction factors and strain: role and social exchange theories. Role theory establishes caregiving as a role and supports theory-driven research and defines the caregiving tasks performed into a specific context of negotiations. The theory also offers insight into the relationship between induction and strain. Social exchange theory offers explanations for the connection between reasons for caregiver selection and strain.

Role Theory

Although role theory originated from an economic perspective and studies of formal organizations, its concepts can be applied to caregiving. "Role relations are seen as a sequence of role bargains and as a continuous process of selection among alternative role behaviors in which each individual seeks to reduce his role strain" (Goode 1960, 483). Role theory assumes norm commitment and institutional integration as society creates roles to maintain order. Individuals learn to manage multiple roles and ensuing role consequences. Early theory states individuals are usually able to fulfill the roles determined by society and family.

Traditional role theorists view multiple role involvements as precursors to role strain, defined as "difficulty in meeting given role demands" (Goode 1960, 485). Early work emphasizes a scarcity approach which suggests strain is experienced when an individual lacks time or energy to fulfill multiple commitments, resulting in role demand overload and conflict which predict role strain. Role strain is the inability to maintain a balanced allocation of limited resources for multiple roles (Goode 1960). Individuals feel obligated to adhere to a norm of adequacy mandated by reference group (society, institutions and families) expectations of the individual. When an individual is unable to allocate available resources to maintain multiple role demands, negative consequences can occur. Role strain is a result of constraints due to competing obligations for time and energy.

Later role theorists question the scarcity hypothesis in deference to an expansion approach—multiple commitments can positively affect individuals (Baruch and Barnett 1986; Marks 1977; Sieber 1974). Expansion theory suggests stress occurs not as a result of the number of roles, but of the quality of role interactions and patterns (Walker, Pratt and Wood 1992). These findings discount a scarcity hypothesis as multiple roles have different effects on women in role overload, conflict and anxiety (Barnett and Baruch 1985). When a woman has multiple role responsibilities, role strain is a normal and expected response (Sieber 1974).

Moreover, later theorists further question the restrictiveness of the early role perspectives. Doress-Worters (1994) is critical of Goode's early work, suggesting the original theory is gender neutral, reminiscent of an earlier, simpler era and is not inclusive of family caregiving roles, particularly those roles which are shared by multiple family members. Further, Doress-Worters (1994) suggests that the number of roles added is not the variable which creates stress, but it is the *type* of role and the value and compensation that is assigned to the additional roles that creates the stressful caregiver response.

Theoretically, assumptions about role accumulation are useful for examining caregiving (Mui 1990). Most caregivers have multiple role commitments which can be compared to "role overload." Competing roles can create conflicts in time and energy, resulting in stress (Stoller and Pugliesi 1989a). Daughter caregivers are candidates for role strain as most have commitments to a spouse, children and employers. Almost two-thirds of daughter caregivers are married, one-fourth have minor children at home and approximately half are employed outside the home (Stone, et al. 1987; U.S. Select Committee on Aging 1987).

Using role theory-driven hypotheses, researchers examine relationships between the quality of the caregiving role and outcomes of caregiving for the caregiver. Findings associate multiple role positions with better health, lower psychological stress and increased self-esteem and well-being (Stoller and Pugliesi 1989a). Caregivers with multiple role obligations experience a buffer effect as other roles enhance well-being, provide resources and links to outside helping networks (Stoller and Pugliesi 1989a). Increases in the number of women's roles can lead to increased perception of competence and positive feelings (Pietromonaco, Manis and Frohardt-Lane 1984). However, multiple obligations create caregiver stress when high levels of care are required (Stoller and Pugliesi 1989a).

Factors thought to be associated with role strain include: 1) frequency of conflict—correlates with presence of caregiver spouse support and minor children in the home (Walker, Pratt and Wood 1992); 2) caregiver perception of elder health as poor; 3) co-residence (Stoller and Pugliesi 1989a); 4) caregiver employment (Orodenker 1990) and, conversely, caregiver unemployment (Spitze, Logan, Joseph and Lee 1994); and 5) elder characteristics (widowed and living alone) (Morycz 1985). An inability to balance role demand overload may result, not only in increased strain, but decreased relationship quality (Scharlach 1987) and a desire for and actual institutionalization of the elder (Morycz 1985).

Regarding gender and strain, Mui (1995) found no gender differences on strain or role overload (studying spousal caregivers), but did note that male caregivers experience higher levels of role conflict. Moreover, Spitze and colleagues (1994) note that men actually experienced higher levels of burden than did women. Furthermore, the female adult daughter caregivers studied by Spitze and colleagues (1994) were found to *not* experience a negative outcome when being responsible for multiple role commitments.

Role theory frames roles as an assumed series of relationships and transactions. This concept can be applied to caregiver induction as "rolemaking between older parents and their adult children is a dynamic process that reflects changing family circumstances" (Hamon and Blieszner 1990, 112). Role theory suggests families determine role assignments (Goode 1960) and responsibility to provide care takes precedence over other obligations (Doty 1986). These expectations determine role assumption and behaviors (Hamon 1988).

Role theory suggests willingness to assume the role is a result of intrinsic gratifications related to role activities, prospective gains and internal self reward/punishment (Goode 1960, 489). This suggests caregivers strive for personal gain to: 1) meet a previous norm expectation, perform caregiving tasks, be cared for in the future and/or receive family or societal approval for assuming the role or 2) avoid criticism by reference groups. A researcher's adherence of the tenets of role theory encourages an examination of the relationship between induction factors and caregiver strain or stress. Research has not specifically established a link between caregiver level of willingness to assume the role and strain, but the theory provides an extension which suggests a research question.

Role theory adds to an explanation of a relationship between caregiver induction and strain as it frames caregiving as an expected role to maintain survival and order of societal institutions. The theory suggests families assume caregivers will integrate a caregiving role into other life commitments and balance caregiving with other roles. The theory suggests strain is a normal response to role demand overload and offers options for reducing strain-manipulation through compartmentalization, delegation and termination.

Role theory has been empirically tested as an explanation for caregiving. Findings, while conflicted, indicate caregiving impact is more complex than previously thought. Evidence suggests it may not just be the accumulation of roles and activities that produce strain/stress, but role quality and context. These findings link caregiver characteristics which predispose the caregiver to be "assigned" the role and his/her response. It is suggested that caregivers will assume the role with a higher level of willingness if the reasons for induction are related to a wish to fulfill a personal need or desire, not as a forced choice.

In sum, role theory is used in this study to associate level of willingness to assume the caregiver role and caregiver strain. The theory suggests unwilling caregivers who assume the role due to a lack of perceived intrinsic gratification become candidates for strain. The theory is being used here to explore the level of strain in persons with a low level of willingness to assume the role.

Social Exchange Theory

Derived from economic theory, social exchange theory encompasses the concepts of exchange, equity and reciprocity and defines caregiving as an exchange of services provided over time. Using this perspective, caregiving is "repaying a debt to the parent or to caring for someone who is considered a part of one's self" (Albert 1990, 320–321). Like economic exchange, the theory assumes: 1) people desire maximum profits and minimum losses; 2) there is no single medium of social exchange; 3) there is no objective, quantifiable system for determining the value of exchanged resources; and 4) exchanges are not assumed to involve reciprocation of the same resource (George 1986). This suggests family relationships are based on reciprocity and exchange in which members engage in numerous, complex acts mixing exchange, equity and role behaviors. Exchange is expected as families are bound by solidarity (no regard for reciprocity), role rights and obligation (George 1986).

Social exchange theory includes the concept of reciprocity (mutual realization of profits) which can motivate exchange (George 1986). As social exchange is an expected or perceived exchange of services, it can determine selection and expectations (Phillips and Rempusheski 1986). The caregiver is selected based on an accumulation of "credits" by the elder with the family member. If the member is indebted to the elder, it becomes his/her duty to reciprocate and fulfill the obligation by providing care regardless of the task needs. Members with financial, emotional or practical debt become candidates for the role.

Reciprocity, payment for services with "credits" earned by the elder for services provided, is a reason for providing care and is related to the amount of help provided (Horowitz and Shindelman 1983). Reciprocity endures over a family's lifetime and results in equitable distribution. Reciprocal exchanges are not time-specific but are a series of interactions which occur through a family life cycle and imply continuation by younger generations (Cantor and Hirshorn 1988). Relationship reciprocity is valued by female caregivers but may be manifested as obligation when a caregiver perceives a lack of reciprocity (Neufeld and Harrison 1992). Feelings regarding anticipation of rewards and indebtedness influence caregiver discomfort. Attempts to eradicate discomfort can result in role induction (Schulz 1990).

Derived from exchange theory, equity is a realization of "equal net gains from the relationship" (George 1986, 72). This suggests a caregiver performs tasks deemed appropriate for exchange of elder-provided services. A negative outcome occurs with service inequity, and the level is comparable to perceived degree of inequity. Caregiver evaluation of outcome is based primarily on the "net" outcome of the experiences versus the positive or negative outcome (Walker, et al. 1995).

Social exchange theory contributes to an explanation of role induction as it views the family as willing and available care providers. Earlier theory frames caregiving as an anomaly or crisis of family life. Exchange theory views it as a normative purchase of service based on accrued credits and not as an isolated event in family life. Current research suggests that elders are actively engaged in social exchange relationships with their adult children (Walker, Pratt and Oppy 1992).

Cultural rules (patterns and traditions determined by a family's racial, ethnic or religious affiliation) influence exchange patterns (Mui 1992). When all other factors are comparable, the issue of "debt" as determined by cultural patterns and traditions becomes a determining factor in induction (Ikels 1983). The complex patterns of exchange over time may prescribe   caregiver identity and role expectations. Theoretically, the caregiver should be an individual who "owes" the elder at the time need arises, received services recently or due to the ongoing nature of exchanges over time. The caregiver should willingly assume the role as a result of an awareness of the existence of "debt." Tasks to be performed should equal those received.

Higher levels of reciprocity are present when the caregiver perceives the relationship with the elder has been and will continue to be an ongoing one for both the caregiver and elder (Chesla, et al. 1994). Conversely, levels of perceived reciprocity are lower in those relationships viewed by the caregiver as being a "transformed" relationship and almost non-existent in relationships perceived to be discontinuous (Chesla, et al. 1994). Of note Chesla and colleagues report that males do not typically perceive their relationships with elders as being continuous and highly reciprocal.

Along with participation in a balanced relationship, cultural rules can determine a secure care plan for the elder (Albert 1990; Wentowski 1981). Security in old age is assured by "buying in" through a major contribution (loan of money, housing or child care). Elders prefer deferred exchange to support familial bonds and insure care (Wentowski 1981). However, exchanges between parents and their adult children vary over time (Spitze and Logan 1992).

Using social exchange theory to test the relationship between filial obligation and parental dependency, Albert (1990) develops categories of caregiver perception of caregiving and parental dependency. Following is a description of the categories developed by Albert:

1) Caregiving as a return to one's parents. This category encompasses concepts of intergenerational reciprocity (parent care of child entitles parent to care; caregiver assumes if he/she provides care, his/her children will do so; and parental and child obligation are similar) and continuity of parent-child roles (parent and child struggle to maintain previous reciprocity but accept elder's increasing dependency).

2) Caregiving as caring for a part of oneself. Intergenerational identity and extreme loyalty is assumed regardless of the previous parent-child relationship. The caregiver assumes he/she is the only person who can provide quality care and may be unable to separate self from parent or role.

Albert suggests the way the caregiver perceives the elder also influences the exchange. The following two categories explain the caregiver perception of the elder's current health status and are later used to establish a correlation between perception of elder and service exchange:

3) The impaired parent is an ill person. Elder need or dependence is a result of normal aging which enables the caregiver to emotionally distance him/herself from caregiving tasks and impending death of the elder.

4) The impaired parent is a child. Caregiver perceives parent care to be similar to child care, thus creating a perceived reversal of roles.

Albert (1990, 327) reports a correlation between caregivers who perceive the parent as ill and those who view caregiving as an exchange of services. This group of caregivers reports lower levels of identity and intimacy with the elder and the role. Caregivers who perceive the elder as a child (high intimacy) also have higher levels of identification with the elder and the role and see caregiving as a part of one's self . Caregivers who perceive caregiving as repaying a debt to the parent view the elder only as ill, while those who feel caregiving is a requirement of a physical bond see the parent as childlike. It is unknown if this positively or negatively affects caregiver response to caregiving.

Motivations for caregiving are noted to be rooted in morals (religion-based) and social (socialization into the caregiving role) (Blieszner and Hamon 1992). These motivations are the outcomes of the family structure and relationships, competing obligations, parental needs and the reconciliation of one's filial expectations and behaviors (Blieszner and Hamon 1992). It is these motivations that determine the adult child's sense of obligation and results in the desire for exchange and reciprocity which occurs with parental caregiving.

Conversely, Jecker (1989) viewing caregiving exchanges from a philosophical perspective, suggests filial duty does not motivate caregiving. Instead, caregiving is simply another of life's experiences in which persons perform services for others with the intention of exchanging or reciprocating other services later. Further, Jecker (1989, 73) suggests "filial duties have no grounding in current moral theory" and adult children are not bound by obligation to respond to all requests made by parents. The adult children may opt to respond to only those requests they choose and they may determine the manner in which they will respond.

Testing social exchange theory and the mother-daughter caregiving relationship, Walker and Allen (1991) suggest exchanges occur which are: 1) intrinsic or rewarding (45%); 2) ambivalent or unbalanced (34%); or 3) conflicted or unrewarding (21%). Daughters who find caregiving rewarding have fewer children and are more likely to reside with the parent while caregiving, while the conflicted group report a history of relationship problems with their mothers, mothers who are more often unmarried by divorce or separation (versus widowhood).

An inappropriate balance of behaviors over time may create conflict and negative outcomes. Conflict, resulting from increased parental dependence on the adult child caregiver, can arise when the caregiving exchanges between parent and child are not perceived as being in balance (Chappell 1990). Ambiguity regarding role assumption can lead to conflict if the exchange is viewed as unbalanced or when the caregiver is no longer certain the norm of solidarity is sufficient to sustain an indefinite commitment to caregiving (George 1986). Further, research has suggested that the caregiving experience can be impacted by issues related to reciprocity (Walker, Pratt and Oppy 1992).

The caregiver's relationship to the elder can impact perceived caregiver reciprocity and strain. Caregivers who perceive the relationship to the elder as less reciprocal (children and non-relatives) report investing more into the relationship than is realized in return. These caregivers report higher levels of stress (Ingersoll-Dayton and Antonucci 1988).

Social exchange theory suggests family "rules" determine which individual owes the elder the most at the time of need, implying induction is overt and voluntary. The theory further suggests tasks performed should be comparable to earlier care. A correlation exists between caregiver perception of parental needs and role assessment (Albert 1990).

Caregiver selection can be motivated by previous or anticipated social exchange. The reason a caregiver assumes the role may subsequently be related to strain experienced. Social exchange theory can be used to explain the relationship between caregiver induction and strain due to the extent of the "debt" the caregiver perceives is owed to the elder. This theory links such reasons for selection as love and feelings of family ties, feelings of duty and obligation, elder request and family tradition (reasons cited by Guberman, et al. 1992). This theory has not been tested but is suggested as caregivers are selected for reasons related to previously incurred debt or anticipated desire for care. These findings suggest caregivers influenced by reasons related to repaying a debt or purchasing future care "credits" will be less stressed.

In sum, caregiver induction varies across families. Few commonalities appear in the literature, suggesting a need for further study. The effects of role induction potentially impact all aspects of caregiving. If one is willing to assume a role, he/she is more likely to experience a positive outcome than if he/she is unwilling. Little is known about how caregiving options are chosen by adult children. While there is no clear consensus, theorists are moving toward accepting caregiving as a normal family life cycle event. Thus, the questions identified in this proposal can aid in examining the relationship between caregiver induction and strain.

RESEARCH QUESTIONS

The aim of this research is to examine the relationship between caregiver strain and two caregiver role induction variables, willingness to assume the role and reasons for selection. The caregiver strain and stress literature suggests that the following factors are related to strain: caregiver race, gender, marital status, relationship to elder, duration of caregiving, caregiver household income and proximity and elder health status. As these factors have empirical support for their influence on caregiver strain, each should serve as a control variable in any examination of the relationship between induction factors and caregiver strain. From the caregiver induction literature, level of willingness to assume the role and reasons for selection emerge as explanatory factors in understanding caregiver strain.

Role theory and social exchange theory suggest a relationship between caregiver level of willingness and reasons for selection and strain. Role theory frames caregiving as a normative role and suggests a relationship that willingness to assume the role may be related to strain. Social exchange theory suggest strain may vary by caregiver reason for selection. Specifically, caregivers motivated to assume the role for reasons related to reciprocity may experience less strain than those caregivers who feel no obligation or need to repay the debt. The caregiving literature does not provide clear guidance for the development of hypotheses; therefore, this study will be exploratory. The following research questions suggest caregiver induction factors are associated with caregiver strain levels:

RESEARCH QUESTION #1
Is the level of willingness to assume the caregiving role associated with caregiver strain?

RESEARCH QUESTION #2
Does caregiver strain differ according to reason for selection?

Variables to be tested include:

DEPENDENT VARIABLE	*LEVEL OF MEASUREMENT*
Level of Caregiver Strain	Continuous

INDEPENDENT VARIABLES

Induction

Level of Willingness	Interval
Reasons for Selection	Categorical

Control Variables*

Race	Dichotomous
Marital Status	Dichotomous
Duration of Caregiving	Continuous

Caregiver Household Income	Continuous
Proximity	Dichotomous
Elder Physical Health Status	Continuous
Elder Mental Status	Continuous

* Two caregiver variables, gender and relationship to the elder will be controlled by study design (to be discussed in Chapter 3).

III
Methodology

SAMPLE

The sample included seventy-one adult daughter primary caregivers caring for chronically ill elderly parents who participated in three ongoing studies. Thirty-eight daughter caregivers were drawn from a study on *Adequacy of Home Care for Chronically Ill Elderly* (Care Plan Study) (Proctor, Morrow-Howell and Chadiha 1990). Nineteen were drawn from a related study, *Increasing the Awareness of Alzheimer's Disease and Assessing the Unmet Needs and Strengths of African-American Caregivers of Elderly Alzheimer's Patients* (Chadiha and Morrow-Howell 1991). An additional sampling source was the *Memory and Aging Project Satellite* (Berg and Edwards 1993). A description of each of the samples is presented in Appendix C. Human subjects approval was obtained from the Washington University Standing Committee on the Use of Human Subjects, the Washington University School of Medicine Human Subjects Committee and the Alzheimer's Disease Research Center Executive Committee.

A power analysis was performed to establish sample size. Using a procedure developed by Borenstein and Cohen (1988), power was calculated for Research Question #1. A correlational analysis was used because the area of interest is the relationship between level of caregiver willingness to assume the role and caregiver strain, when controlling for other variables known to relate to the dependent variable. A correlation of .30 was chosen as a critical effect size. With a sample size of seventy and an alpha level of .05, two-tailed, a power level of .72 results. This suggests a sample of seventy will result in a 72% chance of detecting a population correlation of .30 (a moderate effect size) at the .05 level of significance (Cohen and Cohen, 1983). Although this power level is marginally acceptable, multiple regression, a more powerful statistical procedure, was used.

For Research Question #2, which examines the relationship between the reasons for caregiver selection and caregiver strain, power was calculated for a one-way analysis of variance procedure. This is the appropriate test as the dependent variable is continuous and the independent variable is categorical. It was determined that an effect size of .5 of a point on the Caregiver Strain Index (Robinson 1983) would be practically significant. Using a sample size of seventy with an alpha level of .05, a power level of .987 would result. This suggests that a sample size of seventy will result in a 98% chance of detecting a difference of .5 points between group means at the .05 significance level (Cohen and Cohen 1983).

Respondents in the Care Plan Study reside primarily in the St. Louis metropolitan area and have previously been identified as primary caregivers for non-institutionalized elderly parents diagnosed with congestive heart failure. Respondents were identified by hospital discharge planners and recruited during a hospitalization. Elders and family caregivers were interviewed in the hospital and at home by telephone. The interviews included assessment of functional status, formal and informal caregiving activities, unmet needs and the adequacy of the discharge plan. Interviews were conducted by social work and nursing research assistants.

This sample was used as the caregivers have been identified and have participated in earlier studies. Using this sample builds on existing resources, making it possible to obtain an adequate sample of known daughter caregivers caring for elders with chronic needs. Each participant had accrued at least two years caregiving experience; a period of time that was brief enough to enable the caregiver to recall the induction process as well as to report the caregiver strain currently being experienced. The Care Plan Study sample included a large number (seventy) of daughters serving as primary caregivers and offers variability in proximity, elder health status, age, marital status and socioeconomic status levels. Limitations of this sample included: caregivers may be too distant from induction; sample was limited to congestive heart failure patients only; and was primarily an urban population. These limitations were recognized and were considered in interpreting findings.

Chadiha and Morrow-Howell (1991) used a purposive sample of approximately fifty family caregivers of non-institutionalized African-American elders experiencing cognitive impairment. Respondents were recruited through the Alzheimer's Association, clergy, media and social and health care agencies in a metropolitan area. Interviews matched on race of interviewer were conducted by Dr. Chadiha and social work and psychology graduate student research assistants using a multi-method approach. The approach included qualitative focused audio-taped interviews to assess caregivers' unmet needs and strengths to obtain culturally-specific information. Instruments from the previously described study by Proctor and Morrow-Howell (1990) were used to assess function, needs and caregiving activities using ethnically sensitive items. Strengths of African-American families and the Black church as a source of support to assess at-risk family members' internal and external social support networks were also documented.

As the African-American Caregiver sample was recruited through newspaper ads and referrals, it was recognized that such purposive sampling limits generalizability which is provided by random sampling. The Memory and Aging Project Satellite (MAPS) sample consisted of approximately sixty minority and medically underserved elders and family members in the a metropolitan area. Fifteen of the family members were adult daughters. Elders and family members were interviewed by a nurse for the purpose of primary assessment, diagnosis and case management. The nurse assigns a clinical dementia diagnosis which was confirmed by the Department of Neurology at Regional Hospital. Approximately 75% of this population was African-American; 25% white.

Eligibility criteria for this study include:

1) Caregiver must be a daughter or step-daughter of the elder. While using mixed samples of caregiver types (spouses and non-spouses) can increase generalizability, aggregating data from caregivers with different elder relationships can obscure findings and inaccurately describe the experience (Zarit and Toseland 1989). Limiting this sample to daughter caregivers eliminates the problem of mixing of spouse and non-spouse relationships. It is recognized that the relationships of these caregivers may differ from one other. To test relationships between induction and strain, it is appropriate to use only daughter caregivers who are more likely to provide care to elderly parents, particularly mothers (Stoller 1990). Sons and other non-spouse relatives (including daughters-in-law) are not included in this

sample due to the small numbers of these caregiver categories present in the original samples.

2) Caregiver must have been identified by the elder and herself as the primary caregiver because the purpose of this investigation is to examine the relationship between induction of the primary caregiver and caregiver strain.

3) Caregiver must have been providing at least one caregiving service at the time of the interview. To decrease recall bias and enable the caregiver to accurately describe current caregiving strains, she must have been actively engaged in caregiving. Studies described in the literature consistently include only caregivers currently providing care for these reasons. Caregivers from the original samples no longer providing care due to death, institutionalization, relocation or withdrawal were not eligible.

DESIGN

This study was a cross-sectional survey of adult daughter primary caregivers of elderly parents at varying points in the caregiving experience. Subjects were asked to recall their induction experience to determine the level of willingness to assume the role and reason for selection. While the measurement of induction variables was retrospective, the measurement of caregiver strain was concurrent. An interviewer-administered telephone survey was used for the daughters from the Care Plan Study and Memory and Aging Project Study only as surveys were previously completed for the daughters in the Chadiha and Morrow-Howell study.

QUESTIONNAIRE

The interviewer-administered questionnaire used in Chadiha and Morrow-Howell was replicated for this study. Sections of the instrument used include: Section A (household composition; residence; and length of caregiving); Section C (Caregiver Strain Inventory) (Robinson 1983); Section D (Caregiving tasks; willingness, and reason for selection items); Section E (Caregiver demographics); and Section F (Characteristics of the Elderly Person).

PROCEDURE

From the sample of approximately 300 cases studied by Proctor, Morrow-Howell and Chadiha (1990), seventy of the original sample were adult daughters caregivers. The Chadiha and Morrow-Howell sample included approximately twenty-five daughter caregivers. Data was previously collected by Chadiha and Morrow-Howell and was obtained in the form of a data set. Participants from the Care Plan and Memory and Aging Project studies were contacted to determine eligibility and willingness to participate in this study. A telephone interview was scheduled and conducted with eligible caregivers who agreed to participate. Follow-up telephone calls were made to obtain missing data or clarification of responses. A data set from the Chadiha and Morrow-Howell study was integrated with the information procured by the telephone interviews.

It is recognized that mixed modes of data collection were used. Caregivers in the Chadiha and Morrow-Howell study were interviewed in person, while participants in the Care Plan and Memory and Aging Project studies were interviewed by telephone. Reliability is not generally compromised when data is collected via different methods. Bailey (1978, citing Scott 1961) notes agreement between mailed questionnaires and interviews. Further, Sudman and Bradburn (1982, 263) note agreement in responses to the same questions regardless of type of administration (mail, telephone or personal interview). Using verification of records, underreporting of sensitive information did not differ by method of administration. In fact, overreporting is slightly less in telephone interviews than in face-to-face interviews on questions involving socially desirable behavior. Therefore, the authors suggest "other criteria, including sample biases, ability to ask the required questions, and costs, should usually determine the method of administration." While this mixture should not confound the data, the use of different interviewing methods is noted and will be addressed in the interpretation of findings.

MEASUREMENT

As the sample consisted exclusively of adult daughter caregivers, the variables of gender and relationship to the elder were controlled by study design. Variables statistically controlled included: 1) caregiver race; 2) caregiver marital status; 3) caregiver annual household income (1992); 4) duration of caregiving; 5) caregiver residential proximity to the elder; 6) elder physical health status; and 7) elder mental status. Caregiver age was not included as a design-controlled or statistically-controlled variable as the literature demonstrated that it is the caregiver's relationship to the elder, not age, that impacts stress. The seven control variables were objective measures consistent with the literature. Variables measured are described below.

Independent variables

Caregiver Factors. The following caregiver factors will be described:

1) Level of Willingness. This variable was measured as level of willingness to initially provide care. The willingness measure was taken from the instrument developed by Chadiha and Morrow-Howell (1991). Caregiver-perceived willingness was measured using a 1–5 Likert scale (1 = very unwilling to 5 = very willing). A frequently used scale, the five-level Likert forces the respondent to consider the range of choices without using extreme responses, offers a comparable number of positive and negative options and prevents a simple agree or disagree response (Moser and Kalton 1972). Additionally, five categories are typically the most categories a respondent can recall without the use of a visual cue (card) (Sudman and Bradburn 1982).

2) Reasons for Selection. This variable was measured through the use of an open-ended question in which the caregiver was asked to discuss why she became the primary caregiver. This item was placed at the end of Section D (the third section of the interview) following caregiving arrangements, and caregiver strain items. This section of the interview included the open-ended reason for selection item, followed by the items which addressed the caregiver's level of willingness. The question was asked as: "We would like to learn about how *you* became the primary person to provide care to your (parent). How was the decision made that *you* would be the one responsible for taking care of (parent)." To ensure reliability, only minimal probing was performed. In interviews in which the caregiver appeared to have

difficulty responding to the question, the item was repeated. The responses were recorded verbatim and content analyzed to identify themes and sub-themes within the responses (Guberman, et al. 1992).

Content analysis was conducted using the following procedure:

a. Caregivers' open-ended responses from twenty-one of the interviews conducted by Chadiha and Morrow-Howell were reviewed by four independent reviewers. Each reviewer made notes and developed broad categories of reasons for caregiver selection. Using the guidelines noted in Albert (1990), each reviewer attempted to identify key words and phrases and contextual meaning associated with reasons for selection. In those cases in which the respondent cited more than one reason, the reviewers agreed to identify the reason which appeared to be a primary reason for the caregiver.

b. The reviewers compared categories and established labels and operationalizations for each category. These initial twenty-one responses were then assigned to each category.

3. New responses were assigned to the above categories by three independent raters to establish inter-rater reliability. A kappa coefficient was calculated using Cohen's kappa (Cohen 1960) to determine a chance-corrected reliability estimate for nominal scales. Twenty-two responses were coded by raters #1 and #2 and thirty responses were coded by raters #1 and 3. Using the following formula, an unweighted kappa statistic was derived for responses coded by raters #1 and #2:

$$K = \frac{Po-Pc*}{1-Pc} = \frac{21-1}{22-25} = \frac{.95-.04}{1-.04} = \frac{.91}{.96} = .94$$
$$1-\frac{1}{25}$$

The formula was also applied to the thirty responses coded by raters #1 and #3 to calculate the following kappa statistic:

$$K = \frac{Po-Pc*}{1-Pc} = \frac{25-1}{30-25} = \frac{.83-.04}{1-.04} = \frac{.79}{.96} = .82$$
$$1-\frac{1}{25}$$

* Po—Observed proportion of times that the raters agree

* Pc—Proportion of agreements that are expected to occur by chance alone. Each rater had a one in five chance of selecting one category. Using the multiplication rule for independent events, there is a one in twenty-five chance of both raters obtaining identical results (Pagano 1981).

The five categories of reason for selection that resulted from this process are as follows:

Category #1—REQUEST (n = 17)

a. Explicit request by:	parent (elder)
	parent's spouse
	other family member
	social service agency (to include hospital)
	court system
b. Implicit request by:	parent (elder)
	parent's spouse
	other family member

Examples include:

*"Father asked me to move back. . ."

* ". . . my mother's decision. . ."

* "The courts decided"

* "Social worker called me and asked me"

Category #2—NO OTHER ALTERNATIVE OR RESOURCE
(n = 29)

a. Caregiver perception of lack of available formal or informal options for caregiving. This can be a literal or subjective perception of the unavailability of formal (agency) or informal (family members or other informal groups) caregiving resources.

b. Lack of informal alternatives/resources can include the caregiving being an only child.

c. Relinquishment of responsibility by previous caregiver.

d. Refusal by other family members to provide care.

Examples include:

> * ". . . he had no one else. . ."
> * "I am an only child"
> * "I'm the only immediate living relative in St.Louis"
> * "There was no choice; I was the only one"

Category #3—FAMILY POSITION/STRUCTURE (n = 9)

a. Caregiver's position within the family (chronological age and gender can contribute to caregiver's perception of her responsibilities to the elder).

b. Caregiver's position may be related to her availability to provide care. For example, the eldest may not have competing commitments (young children, employment, etc.) which would enable her to assume the caregiving role.

c. Position may also relate to the "family's culture." Specifically, the eldest or the youngest may be "expected" by the family to provide care because of her position and status within the family.

Examples include:

> * "I am the oldest daughter. . . took early retirement"
> * "I am the youngest child. . . it fell on me. . ."
> * "I was the only one who could do it. . . I'm the oldest. . ."

Category #4—DUTY AND/OR OBLIGATION (n = 4)

a. Caregiver perception of her responsibility or desire to provide care resulting from the relationship history with the elder. Reasons for role assumption can include:

duty, obligation, love, affection and/or reciprocation of earlier care

Examples include:

* "... I felt I should do it. . ."
* "She's my mother and I felt I should do it. . ."
* "... I feel responsible. . ."
* "... we felt obligated"

Category #5—OTHER (n = 12)

This category includes two primary reason areas:

a. Reasons related to caregiver's self-decision to assume the caregiving role.

Examples include:

* "I decided to do it on my own"
* "It's just my nature"
* "I just picked it up"

b. Reasons related to caregiver's geographic proximity to the elder.

Examples include:

* "I'm the closest"
* "I was just the closest one (within three miles)"
* "It was convenient. . ."

A sample of the responses to reason for selection have been grouped by category. The category groups may be found in Appendix D.

Following the content analysis of this variable and data coding, further study of the "other" category revealed that the category could be further delineated and potentially re-labelled in an effort to clarify and strengthen this category. Therefore, following a review of each of the "other" responses, the following re-assignments were initiated:

1) Two responses previously assigned to "other" were re-assigned to the second category, no other alternative. These responses were:

> "My brothers live up north. . . my sister helped to a point, but not much."
> "There was no one else."
> ". . . she has five girls and I think they should share the care, but they won't."

2) Three responses previously assigned to "other" were re-assigned to the first category, request by parent or other. These responses were:

> "She's dependent on us."
> "I was close to him. . . I moved in when my mother had cancer."
> "It wasn't really me. I was still in high school and I started driving her to appointments."

3) The remaining responses in the "other" category were re-labelled as caregiver self-decision to provide care. Those responses which Identified caregiver proximity to elder as a primary reason for selection into the caregiving role were reassigned to other categories if the response suggested a second theme. Those responses in which proximity was the only theme were maintained in the self-decision category. Based on a review of caregiver responses, it appears other alternatives apparently do exist in those situations, but the caregiver has *chosen* to provide care as she is physically the closest candidate to the elderly parent.

Conceptual and empirical reasons were identified which warranted collapsing two of the categories of the variable, reason for selection. Conceptually, family structure was combined with duty and obligation to provide care as position in the family may imply one's sense of duty and obligation to family. Specifically, the birth order position one holds in the family may implicitly or explicitly carry with it an expectation for caregiving responsibility. For example, in some families eldest daughters may perceive an expectation that because they are the oldest, they are responsible for providing care to the parent(s). Other families, however, may have similar "rules" regarding expectations of family members as determined by position in the family, but apply differently depending on position (younger, males versus females, etc.). Empirically, the number of observations in these two categories was too small for multivariate analysis. Further, the means of caregiver stress were compared and no statistically significant differences were found between these two groups. The mean stress level for Category #3—Family Structure is 10.8; the mean stress level for Category #4—Duty/Obligation is 9.3 (t = -0.8973, p< 0.3888). This variable was, thus, collapsed from a five-level categorical variable to a four-level categorical variable.

Control Variables

Two variables, caregiver gender and relationship to elder, were controlled by study design as all participants were adult daughters. Seven variables were statistically controlled:

Caregiver Race. This variable was measured dichotomously as white and African-American. This measure was added to the instrument for the telephone surveys as it was not included on the original survey instrument.

Marital Status—measured by category of martial status: a) married, b) separated, c) divorced, d) widowed, e) never married or f) common-aw married. For analysis, this variable was collapsed to a dichotomous variable (married and not married).

Caregiver marital status—originally measured using eight categories. Since the literature suggests there are no differences in the caregiving behaviors of non-married caregivers, the variable was collapsed into a dichotomous variable (married and not married).

Caregiver Household Income–measured by caregiver responses to a question of total 1992 caregiver gross household income (twenty-two income categories).

Duration of Caregiving—measured continuously as number of days, weeks or years caregiver has provided care to elder.

Proximity—measured dichotomously as caregiver residence or non-residence with the elder.

Elder Physical Health Status—measured by caregiver perception of elder physical health status using a portion of the standardized measure developed by Blessed, Tomlinson and Roth (1968). Caregivers responded to a four-level Likert scale regarding the elder's physical health.

Elder Mental Status—measured using a portion of the Blessed instrument. Two of the three sections of the Blessed Dementia Scale were incorporated: 1) Changes in Performance of Everyday Activities and 2) Changes in Habits. A summative score was derived from responses to the following items:

1) Changes in Performance of Everyday Activities—three level Likert ratings (0 = no ability; 1 = some ability; and 2 = all ability) are assigned to each of the following instrumental activities of daily living: household tasks, money management, information or event recall, ability to move about in familiar environments, ability to comprehend information and tendency to dwell in the past.

2) Changes in Habits—three and four level Likert scales are used to measure the following activities of daily living: eating; dressing; and toileting.

Dependent Variable

Caregiver Strain was measured here by the commonly used Caregiving Strain Inventory (Robinson 1983) (used in Chadiha and Morrow-Howell). This thirteen-item dichotomous inventory was designed to assess caregiver-perceived strain. As mentioned in Chapter 1, Robinson adopted the definition of stress offered by Pearlin and Schooler (1978) and developed a measure of objective caregiver strain. Building on the earlier work of Robinson and Thurnher (1979), this screening instrument was developed to identify caregiver strain as a first step in targeting potential risks for the elder and caregiver. The Index was developed in conjunction with a hospital home care program for use in planning elders' hospital discharges (Personal communication with Dr. Robinson 1993).

This thirteen-item dichotomous instrument is scored by summing the "yes" responses. Dichotomous items ease caregiver understanding and response. The scale includes items which address multiple facets of caregiving (elder characteristics, subjective perception of caregiving, and caregiver's emotional status). The inventory includes questions about the caregiver current caregiving experience in the areas of: sleep disturbance; physical and emotional strain; inconvenience; family, personal, emotional and work adjustments resulting from caregiving demands; care-recipient personality changes and behavioral disruptions; and feeling overwhelmed. Scores in the validation effort ranged from 0–12 with a mean of 3.519 (SD = 3.497). A later administration of the instrument with caregivers of demented elders was 8.0 (Personal communication with Dr. Robinson 1993). A score of seven or more suggests a "greater level of strain."

The instrument was validated using a sample of eighty-five caregivers of non-institutionalized elders (65+ years) two months after a hospitalization for heart disease or hip fracture. The majority of elders (88.1%) did not exhibit cognitive impairment; two-thirds were in good or excellent health; and 71.2% were independent in activities of daily living. Strain is measured in three areas: elder characteristics; caregivers' subjective perceptions of the caregiving relationship; and caregiver physical and emotional health. Internal consistency as measured by Cronbach's alpha is adequate (.86). This value did not increase when any one of the items was eliminated from the scale.

Findings reported in the article describing the validation effort include: no significant gender differences noted; caregiver relationship to elder was not significantly related to caregiver strain; no significant differences are noted for variations in caregiver health status or residence; and significant correlations between employment and strain. Racial differences for this measure are unknown. Moderate positive correlations were found between the caregiver strain score and elder age, re-admission to the hospital and mental status. Negative correlations occurred with elder functional status and satisfaction with recovery.

ANALYSIS

Univariate statistics was used to describe the sample. A SAS univariate procedure and frequencies was performed on the dependent and control variables—caregiver race, marital status, annual caregiver household income, duration of caregiving, caregiver residential proximity to the elder and elder physical health status and elder mental status—and the two independent variables—level of willingness and reasons for selection—to determine distribution, normality of distribution and representativeness across groups. Transformations were performed, as needed, to adjust for non-normality before proceeding to bivariate analysis.

Separate analyses were performed for the research questions:

RESEARCH QUESTION #1
   Is the level of willingness to assume the caregiving role associated with caregiver strain?

Following univariate analysis, bivariate analysis (primarily zero-order correlations, t-tests and analyses of variance (ANOVA's) as determined by level of measurement) were performed to determine relationships between the independent variables and the dependent variable. A bivariate analysis was performed with the independent and control variables and the dependent variable, caregiver strain. A check for multicollinearity was performed to determine if any of the independent and control variables were highly correlated with one another. The bivariate relationships were examined for curvilinearity.

The research question were tested by regressing the dependent variable, caregiver strain, on the independent variable, level of willingness, and the control variables to determine the relationship between the independent variable and the dependent variable in the controlled setting. The following ordinary least squares regression was performed:

DEPENDENT VARIABLE   INDEPENDENT VARIABLES
Caregiver Strain   =   (Race + Marital Status + Caregiver
                             Household Income + Duration +
                             Proximity + Elder Physical Health
                             Status + Elder Mental Health
                             Status) + Level of Willingness

Results were examined for statistical significance (p<.05) and significant parameter estimates was assessed in terms of magnitude and direction.

RESEARCH QUESTION #2
Does caregiver strain differ according to reason for selection?

Bivariate analyses determined the presence of statistically significant relationships between the independent variable, reasons for selection, and the control variables (race, marital status, socioeconomic status, duration of caregiving, proximity and elder physical and mental status) and the dependent variable, caregiver strain. Analyses of variance were performed to determine differences between group means for reason for selection. Problems with multicollinearity were addressed after inspection of correlations between the independent and control variables.

Multiple regression was used to examine the research question. The dependent variable, caregiver strain, was regressed on the independent variable, reasons for selection, and the control variables (race, marital status, socioeconomic status, proximity, elder physical health status and elder mental status) to determine the presence of a statistically significant relationship (p<.05) between the independent variable and the dependent variable in the controlled setting. The following regression was performed:

DEPENDENT VARIABLE   INDEPENDENT VARIABLES
Caregiver Strain   =   (Race + Marital Status + Caregiver
                             Household Income + Duration +
                             Proximity + Elder Physical Health
                             Status + Elder Mental Health
                             Status) + Reasons for Selection

Using the GLM procedure in SAS ordinary least squares regression can incorporate both continuous and categorical variables (SAS Manual 1988). In the regression model, reasons for selection was maintained in four level form and entered last for analysis, similar to an analysis of covariance. Post hoc least squares means test compared mean level of strain between categories, controlling for the other variables in the model.

IV
Results

This chapter will present the results from this research effort. Findings to be presented include: sample description, sample description by the source (group of caregivers, to be described) from which the data was collected, bivariate relationships and multivariate relationships.

DESCRIPTION OF SAMPLE

The sample included seventy-one adult daughters who were serving as primary caregivers of elderly parents at the time of interview. Caregiver sample characteristics are described in Table 1. The mean age for caregivers in this sample was 51.06 years (SD = 10.36; skew = 0.11) with the ages ranging from 28–79 years. Approximately seventy percent of the caregiver sample was African-American and approximately thirty percent was White. Less than half (45.1%) was married and the same percentage co-resided with the elderly parent. The average educational level for caregivers was 12.82 years (SD = 3.21; skew = -1.37). Most of the caregivers were employed full or part–time (62%). The mean annual caregiver household income for 1992 was 12.2 on a scale of 1 to 22 with the 12th interval representing $17,000–$19,999/year. Thirteen caregivers refused to respond to the question regarding household income, leaving a sample size of fifty-eight on this variable. Management of this issue is further discussed in the section regarding missing values. The average caregiver had been providing care to the elderly parent just less than six years (mean = 70.35 months; SD = 66.35 months; skew = 3.22) with a range of nine to 456 month.

TABLE 1
CAREGIVER SAMPLE CHARACTERISTICS

CAREGIVER
CHARACTERISTICS

Variable	Frequency	Percent
Race		
Black	50	70.4%
White	21	29.6%
Marital Status		
Married	32	45.1%
Not Married	39	54.9%
Employment Status		
Employed	44	62.0%
Unemployed	14	19.7%
Retired	12	16.9%
Other*	1	1.4%
Residential Proximity		
Co-resident	32	45.1%
Non-co-resident	39	54.9%

	Mean	Std. Dev.	Range	Skew
Caregiver Household Income (1992) (n = 58)	12.12	6.73	1–22	-0.395
Age (in years)	51.06	10.36	28–79	0.11
Education (in years)	12.82	3.21	0–17	-1.37
Duration of Caregiving (months)	70.35	66.35	9–456	3.22

* Other—professional volunteer

TABLE 2
ELDER SAMPLE CHARACTERISTICS

ELDER CHARACTERISTICS					
Variable	Frequency	Percent			
Gender					
Male	15	21.1%			
Female	56	78.9%			
Marital Status					
Married	17	23.9%			
Divorced	5	7.0%			
Widowed	48	67.6%			
Never Married	1	1.4%			
Physical Health Status					
Very Good	11	15.5%			
Good	14	19.7%			
Fair	30	42.3%			
Poor	16	22.5%			
		Mean	Std. Dev.	Range	Skew
Age (in years)		79.39	6.60	67–99	0.37
Mental Status		10.28	3.85	1–17*	-0.33

* Higher scores indicate higher levels of cognitive impairment

Elder characteristics are described in Table 2. The majority of the elders in this sample are women (78.9%) and widowed (67.6%). Elder age ranged from 67–99 years with the mean age of elders being 79.39 years (SD = 6.68; skew = 0.37). Almost half (42.3%) of the elders were perceived by the caregiver as having only a fair physical health status. Over one-third of the elders were viewed by their caregivers as being in good or very good physical health, while one-fifth (22.5%) were thought to be in poor health by their primary caregivers.

Using a modified version of the Blessed Mental Status instrument, the mean level of caregiver-perceived elder mental status was 10.28 (SD = 3.85) on a scale ranging from 1–17, with higher scores indicating a moderate level of cognitive impairment.

Using the categories developed for the independent variable, reason for selection, the primary reason for selection perceived by the caregiver was no other alternative existed for care (40.8%) followed by request by parent or other (23.9%), caregiver self-decision (16.9%), family structure and duty/obligation (18.3%–12.7% and 5.6%, respectively).

Caregiver perception of the level of willingness to assume the caregiving role ranged from 1 (unwilling) to 5 (very willing) with the mean level of willingness being 4.53 (SD = 0.95; skew = -2.19). The distribution of this variable is skewed, in part due to the large number of responses in the high range of the level of willingness to provide care. Due to the skew, this variable was collapsed (see later discussion). The findings from the univariate analysis of the independent variables are presented in Table 3.

The Robinson Caregiver Strain Index (1983) was used to measure caregiver strain. The scores on the Caregiver Strain Index can range from 0–13 with higher scores indicating more caregiver strain. The mean caregiver strain level was 8.21 (SD = 3.65 and skew = -0.415). The dependent variable is described in Table 4.

TABLE 3
DESCRIPTION OF INDEPENDENT VARIABLES

INDEPENDENT VARIABLE	Frequency	Percent
Reason for Selection		
Request	17	23.9%
No Alternative	29	40.8%
Family Structure and Duty and		
Obligation	13	18.3%
Self-decision	12	16.9%

	Mean	Std. Dev.	Range	Skew
Level of Willingness	4.53	0.954	1–5*	-2.188

* Higher score indicates higher level of willingness

TABLE 4
DESCRIPTION OF DEPENDENT VARIABLE

DEPENDENT VARIABLE	Mean	Std. Dev.	Range	Skew
Caregiver Strain	8.211	3.652	0–13*	-0.415

* Higher score indicates higher level of caregiver strain

The sample is described by the data source from which the data was collected. The groups will be presented here in the order of: African-American study, Care Plan study and Memory and Aging Project Study study. Tables 5 (caregiver characteristics), 6 (elder characteristics) and 7 (independent and dependent variables) provide a complete description of these data and the statistical tests used to determine if the three samples differ.

To determine if the three sample sources differed statistically ($p < .05$) from one another, each of the variables was tested using the appropriate procedure for the level of measurement. Bivariately, the variables found to be statistically different by source include: caregiver race (X^2 = 11.1; df = 2), caregiver employment (F = 12.13; df = (2,68)), caregiver residential proximity (X^2 = 12.16; df = 2), elder physical health status (F = 4.44; df = (2,68)), elder mental status (F = 17.18; df = (2,68)) and caregiver level of willingness to assume the role (X^2 = 6.049; df = 2). Statistically significant differences were not noted in the remaining caregiver variables (marital status, annual household income, duration of caregiving or age), elder variables (gender, marital status or age), the second independent variable, reason for selection, or the dependent variable, caregiver strain.

TABLE 5
CAREGIVER CHARACTERISTICS

VARIABLE	AFRICAN-AMERICAN STUDY (N = 19)	CARE PLAN STUDY (N = 38)	MEMORY AND AGING PROJECT SATELLITE STUDY (N = 14)	BIVARIATE TEST OF DIFFERENCES BY SOURCE
Race				
Black	19 (100%)	22 (57.9%)	5 (35.7%)	$X^2 = 11.1*$
White	0 (0%)	16 (42.1%)	9 (64.3%)	df = 2
Marital Status				
Married	8 (42.1%)	18 (47.4%)	6 (42.9%)	$X^2 = 0.176$
Not Married	11 (57.9%)	20 (52.6%)	8 (57.1%)	df = 2
Employment Status				
Employed	5 (26.3%)	27 (71.1%)	12 (85.7%)	$F = 12.13*$
Unemployed	5 (26.3%)	8 (21.1%)	1 (7.1%)	df = (2,68)
Retired	8 (42.1%)	3 (7.9%)	1 (7.1%)	
Other*	1 (5.3%)	0 (0.0%)	0 (0.0%)	
Proximity				
Co-resident	4 (21.1%)	13 (34.2%)	4 (28.6%)	$X^2 = 12.16*$
Non-co-resident	15 (78.9%)	25 (65.8%)	10 (71.4%)	df = 2

TABLE 5 (cont'd)
CAREGIVER CHARACTERISTICS

VARIABLE	AFRICAN-AMERICAN STUDY	CARE PLAN STUDY	MEMORY AND AGING PROJECT SATELLITE STUDY	BIVARIATE TEST OF DIFFERENCES BY SOURCE
Household Income (1992) (N = 58)				
Mean	11.06	12.64	12.38	$F = .30$
Standard Deviation	7.07	6.76	6.58	$df = (2,55)$
Range	1–22	1–22	1–22	
Sample Size	17	28	13	
Age (in years)				
Mean	54.42	49.58	50.50	$F = 1.42$
Standard Deviation	11.79	9.94	9.01	$df = (2,68)$
Range	33–79	28–75	30–62	

TABLE 5 (cont'd)
CAREGIVER CHARACTERISTICS

VARIABLE	AFRICAN-AMERICAN STUDY	CARE PLAN STUDY	MEMORY AND AGING PROJECT SATELLITE STUDY	BIVARIATE TEST OF DIFFERENCES BY SOURCE
Duration (months)				
Mean	60.47	68.26	89.43	F = 0.25[1]
Standard Deviation	45.50	50.50	114.16	df = (2,68)
Range	12–156	18–252	9–456	
Education (years)				
Mean	12.84	12.53	13.57	F = 0.54
Standard Deviation	1.98	3.67	3.27	df = (2,68)
Range	9–17	0–17	8–17	

* p<.05 [1] Inferential test performed on logged values (see page 73 for discussion)

TABLE 6
ELDER SAMPLE CHARACTERISTICS BY SOURCE

VARIABLE	AFRICAN-AMERICAN STUDY(N = 19)	CARE PLAN STUDY (N = 38)	MEMORY AND AGING PROJECT SATELLITE (N = 14)	BIVARIATE SOURCE
Gender				
Male	1 (5.3%)	10 (26.3%)	4 (28.6%)	$X^2 = 3.95$
Female	18 (94.7%)	28 (73.7%)	10 (71.4%)	df = 2
Marital Status				
Married	8 (42.1%)	7 (18.4%)	2 (14.3%)	F = 1.52
Divorced	0 (0.0%)	3 (7.9%)	2 (14.3%)	df = (2.68)
Widowed	10 (52.6%)	28 (73.7%)	10 (71.4%)	
Never Married	1 (5.3%)	0 (0.0%)	0 (0.0%)	
Physical Health Status				
Very Good	2 (10.5%)	12 (31.6%)	2 (14.3%)	$X^2 = 4.44*$
Good	9 (47.4%)	17 (44.7%)	4 (28.6%)	df = (2.68)
Fair	3 (15.8%)	7 (18.4%)	4 (28.6%)	
Poor	5 (26.3%)	2 (5.3%)	4 (28.6%)	

TABLE 6 (cont'd)
ELDER SAMPLE CHARACTERISTICS BY SOURCE

VARIABLE	AFRICAN-AMERICAN STUDY(N=19)	CARE PLAN STUDY (N=38)	MEMORY AND AGING PROJECT SATELLITE N=14)	BIVARIATE SOURCE
Age				
Mean	79.47	78.84	80.79	$F = 0.44$
Standard Deviation	5.46	7.51	5.47	$df = (2.68)$
Range	67–88	68–99	72–92	
Mental Status				
Mean	7.00	12.18	9.57	$F = 17.18*$
Standard Deviation	2.60	2.98	4.29	$df = (2.68)$
Range	1–11	4–17	3–13	

$* p < .05$

TABLE 7
INDEPENDENT AND DEPENDENT VARIABLES BY SOURCE

VARIABLE	AFRICAN-AMERICAN STUDY (N = 19)	CARE PLAN STUDY (N = 38)	MEMORY AND AGING PROJECT SATELLITE STUDY (N = 14)	BIVARIATE SOURCE
Reason for Selection				
Request	7 (36.8%)	7 (18.4%)	3(21.4%)	X² = 2.93
No Alternative	7 (36.8%)	16 (42.1%)	6(42.9%)	df = 6
Structure, Duty or Obligation	2 (10.5%)	8 (21.1%)	3(21.4%)	
Self-Decision	3 (15.8%)	7 (18.4%)	2(14.3%)	
Level of Willingness[1]				
Mean	4.68	4.58	4.21	F = 3.17*
Standard Deviation	0.94	0.95	0.97	df = (2,68)
Range	1–5	1–5	1–5	
Caregiver Strain				
Mean	9.16	7.66	8.43	F = 1.10
Standard Deviation	3.98	3.53	3.50	df = (2,68)
Range	0–13	2–13	3–13	

* p < .05 [1] Inferential test performed on collapsed dichotomous level (see page 73 for discussion)

BIVARIATE RELATIONSHIPS

Transformation of Variables for Analysis

In order to meet the assumptions of the bivariate and multivariate analyses to be performed, three variable required transformations. The transformations are described below.

Log Transformation. As reported previously, the control variable, duration of caregiving, was noted to be extremely skewed. The skew was found to be a result of positive outliers. Therefore, a log transformation was performed to bring this variable into a more acceptable range for multivariate analysis (Kruskal 1968). Following the implementation of a log transformation procedure, the univariate analysis yielded the following results:

Mean	.93
Standard Deviation	0.80
Range	2.19–6.12
Skew	0.13

The skew of the variable is now within acceptable limits for an assumption of normality. From this point on, the logged version of the variable will be presented.

Collapsing of Variables. Level of willingness was collapsed from a five-level continuous variable to a two-level dichotomous variables of unwilling (1) and willing (2). The unwilling category includes responses from categories 1 (very unwilling), 2 (somewhat unwilling) and 3 (neutral). The willing category includes the remaining responses in categories 4 (somewhat willing) and 5 (very willing). After collapsing this variable, most caregivers remain in the willing category (84.5%) with 15.5% in the unwilling category. This variable was collapsed due to the small number of observations in several of the levels. Additionally, the skew on the original five-level variable was sufficiently large to violate the assumptions of normality.

Missing Values. As noted previously, thirteen respondents refused to provide information regarding the annual income of the caregiver household. In order to preserve the total sample size of seventy-one observations, it was determined that the missing data on this variable could be extrapolated from data collected elsewhere in the interview. A traditional measure of socioeconomic status, such as the original Hollingshead Two Factor Index of Social Position (Hollingshead 1957), was not used due to measurement stability problems. The original Hollingshead Index, for example, has become unstable in recent years due to increases in new occupations and women's labor force participation (Haug 1973). This instability can detract from the reliability of the measure and lead to measurement error. Measuring household income can enable women's labor force participation to be recognized. A status score using the more recent Hollingshead Four Factor Index of Social Status (1975) which includes the factors of education, occupation, gender and marital status could not be estimated due to the fact these data were not collected on other household members.

The first step in assigning values to the missing data was to reduce the number of categories of annual caregiver household income. Based on the univariate analysis of the sample of fifty-eight, the original twenty-two income categories were collapsed to four levels as suggested by the frequency distribution. The collapsed levels included the following ranges of annual income for each caregiver household: 1) Less than $10,999, 2) $11,000–$19,999, 3) $20,000–$39,999 and 4) $40,000 and above.

Data from the variables measuring caregiver occupation, employment status, education and marital status were reviewed for each of the observations missing this information. The decision was made using the information described in each of these items to assign income ranges to one of four levels for each of the missing values by incorporating this data. Using the data from these four items, caregiver annual household income was assigned to one of the four categories described above. For example, if a caregiver was married and employed, her annual income category was assigned to the third category.

Univariate and correlational analyses were performed on the sample of 71 observations. Results include: Mean = 2.5; Standard Deviation = 1.14; Skew = -0.15; Zero-order correlation with education (r) = 0.40 (p<.0006), as compared to a correlation of .32 on the original data, using fifty-one observations. For multivariate analysis, this variable will be considered as a four-level variable.

Independent Variables with Dependent Variable. Bivariate relationships between the independent variables noted in the research questions and the dependent variable, caregiver strain, were tested using the appropriate procedures. Results are presented in Table 8. Zero-order correlations were performed for the continuous variables: caregiver household income (collapsed) ($r = 0.195$; $p = 0.142$), duration of caregiving (logged) ($r = 0.134$; $p = 0.263$),elder mental status ($r = -0.104$; $p = 0.389$) and elderly physical health status ($r = -0.040$; $p=0.738$). T-tests were performed on the dichotomous variables: caregiver race ($t = 0.323$; $p = 0.748$), caregiver marital status ($t = -0.374$; $p = 0.710$), caregiver residential proximity ($t = -1.669$; $p = 0.100$) and caregiver level of willingness to assume the role ($t = 1.05$; $p = 0.298$). An F value was obtained for the categorical variable, reason for selection ($F = 2.23$; $df = (3.67)$; $p = 0.092$). No variables in this analysis were found to be statistically significant at the .05 level.

Despite the lack of statistical significance at the bivariate level, a multivariate analysis was conducted to fulfill the original intention of the research: to test the independent variables of interest when controlling for variables suggested in the literature to be related to caregiver strain. Additionally, this ensures that suppression is not operating between any two independent variables (Cohen and Cohen 1983).

TABLE 8
BIVARIATE RELATIONSHIPS BETWEEN INDEPENDENT
VARIABLES AND CAREGIVER STRAIN

VARIABLE	Correlation		T-test		F-test
			TYPE OF TEST		
Caregiver Race			t = 0.323		
Caregiver Marital			p = 0.748		
Status			t = -0.374		
Caregiver			p = 0.710		
Residential			t = -1.669		
Proximity			p = 0.100		
Caregiver					
Household	r =	0.395			
Income (N = 58)	p =	0.142			
Duration of					
Caregiving	r =	0.134			
(logged)	p =	0.263			
Elder Physical	r =	-0.040			
Health Status	p =	0.738			
Elder Mental	r =	-0.104			
Status	p =	0.389			
					F = 2.23
Reason for					df = (3,67)
Selection					p = 0.092
Level of			t = 1.05		
Willingness			p = 0.298		

Multicollinearity Check. In preparation for multiple regression, zero-order correlations were performed as an initial test of multicollinearity (Morrow-Howell 1994). These findings are presented in Table 9. No indication of multicollinearity was noted. As a more stringent test of multicollinearity at the multivariate level, a variance inflation factor test was performed and will be discussed further in the section on regression diagnostics.

Curvilinearity Check. In preparation for multiple regression, assumptions of linearity were tested. Plots of the continuous independent variables versus the dependent variable were performed. No evidence of curvilearity was detected; therefore, the assumptions of linearity were accepted.

TABLE 9
RELATIONSHIPS BETWEEN INDEPENDENT VARIABLES (Initial Multicollinearity Check)

Variable	Caregiver Race	Caregiver Marital Status	Caregiver Proximity	Income	Duration of Care	Elder Health Status	Elder Mental Status	Level of Willingness
Caregiver Race	r = 1.000 p = 0.00							
Caregiver Marital Status	r = 0.281 p = 0.017*	r = 1.000 p = 0.000						
Caregiver Proximity	r = 0.277 p = 0.019*	r = 0.081 p = 0.502	r = 1.000 p = 0.000					
Caregiver Household Income	r = -0.278 p = 0.035*	r = -0.381 p = 0.003*	r = -0.097 p = 0.468	r = 1.000 p = 0.000				
Duration of care	r = -0.093 p = 0.439	r = -0.006 p = 0.962	r = -0.031 p = 0.799	r = -0.201 p = 0.130	r = 1.000 p = 0.000			
Elder Physical Health	r = 0.249 p = 0.036*	r = 0.087 p = 0.471	r = 0.346 p = 0.003*	r = -0.054 p = 0.688	r = -0.121 p = 0.315	r = 1.000 p = 0.000		
Elder Mental Status	r = -0.009 p = 0.942	r = 0.052 p = 0.668	r = -0.229 p = 0.054*	r = 0.002 p = 0.988	r = 0.065 p = 0.591	r = -0.261 p = 0.028*	r = 1.000 p = 0.000	
Level of Willingness	r = -0.022 p = 0.858	r = 0.160 p = 0.183	r = -0.003 p = 0.978	r = -0.256 p = 0.052	r = 0.079 p = 0.514	r = -0.115 p = 0.339	r = -0.009 p = 0.940	r = 1.000 p = 0.000

*$p < .05$

MULTIVARIATE RELATIONSHIPS

Testing for Data Source Differences

A multivariate test of the relationship between data source and the dependent variable, caregiver strain, was conducted. Caregiver strain was regressed on the control variables (caregiver race, marital status, proximity, household income, duration of caregiving, elder physical health status and elder mental status), the independent variable of interest (level of willingness to assume the role or reason for selection into the caregiving role) and a variable indicating data source (African-American Study, Care Plan Study or Memory and Aging Project Study). When testing the relationship between level of willingness to provide care and caregiver strain, the F statistic was 1.51 (p<0.14). When testing the relationship between reason for selection and caregiver strain, the F statistic was 1.20 (p<0.31). Given that sample source was not significant, it was eliminated from further multivariate analyses.

Multivariate Analysis of the Relationship Between Level of Willingness and Caregiver Strain

Multivariately, the relationship between level of willingness to provide care and caregiver strain was tested using an ordinary least squares multiple regression procedure. The dependent variable, caregiver strain, was regressed on the independent variable, level of willingness to assume the caregiving role, controlling for caregiver race, marital status, residential proximity, household income and duration of caregiving and elder factors of physical health and mental status.

The findings are presented in Table 10. No variables in the examination of this relationship were found to be statistically significant at the .05 level. However, caregiver residential proximity to the elder was marginal (p<0.09) as was caregiver annual household income (p<0.09). The adjusted R-square was 0.0436, accounting for only 4% of the variance in the regression model.

Regression Diagnostic Analysis. The variance inflation factors were calculated as a more rigorous test of multicollinearity. A higher value indicates more multicollinearity. When using Fox's guidelines

(Fox 1991), no problems with multicollinearity were detected. An analysis of the error terms was performed. Results indicated the error terms are normally distributed (skew = -0.21).

To examine homoscedasticity, the predicted values were plotted against the error terms. The points appeared randomly distributed with no patterns noted. Thus, there is no evidence of homoscedasticity.

Additional Exploratory Analysis. Three additional regression analyses were performed to explore the relationship between the level of willingness to assume the caregiving role and caregiver strain. First, a "leaps and bounds" procedure, an option within the SAS regression procedure, was performed. This procedure tests every possible combination of independent variables and identifies the model with the most predictive power and the least increment to the R-square simply due to the number of variables. No model using this procedure reaches statistical significance (p<.05). However, the findings indicate the best model includes: caregiver residential proximity, caregiver marital status, caregiver household income, duration of caregiving and elder physical health status. Of these variables, only caregiver residential proximity is marginally significant.

Secondly, a leaps and bounds regression procedure was performed with a reduced number of variables which included caregiver level of willingness to assume the caregiving role and five control variables, race, caregiver residential proximity to the elder, caregiver househole income, elder physical health status and elder mental status. Again, as in the previous leaps and bounds procedure, no model reaches statistical significance. The best model was a five-variable model which included: caregiver residential proximity to the elder; caregiver household income; elder physical status; elder mental status; and level of willingness to assume the role. Only caregiver residential proximity to the elder reaches marginal statistical significance (p<0.0777).

A third regression procedure was performed using five control variables and the independent variable, level of willingness to assume the caregiving role. The results are presented in Table 11. The control variables included were: race, caregiver residential proximity to elder, caregiver household income, elder physical health status and elder mental status. These variables were retained as the literature suggests race, elder physical health status and elder mental status have the strongest relationships with caregiver strain. Caregiver residential proximity and caregiver household income were retained as both were marginally significant in the previous analysis. The results indicate marginal statistical significance for only caregiver residential proximity.

Analysis was performed to detect the presence of interactions between the independent variables in this model and the dependent variable, caregiver strain. No interactions were noted.

TABLE 10
MULTIPLE REGRESSION OF THE RELATIONSHIP BETWEEN
THE LEVEL OF WILLINGNESS AND CAREGIVER STRAIN

Analysis of Variance

Source	DF	Sum of Squares	Mean Square	F Value	Prob>F	Adjusted R square
Model	8	142.773	17.847	1.399	0.2150	0.0436
Error	62	791.058	12.759			
C Total	70	933.831				

Paranmeter Estimates

Variable	DF	Parameter Estimate	Standard Error	T for HO: Parameter = 0	Prob >|T|	Variance Inflation
Intercept	1	5.574401	4.36558645	1.277	0.2064	0.0000000
Race	1	-0.280439	1.05380987	-0.266	0.7910	1.2871781
Proximity	1	1.596882	0.94871718	1.683	0.0974	1.2399750
Marital Status	1	1.310556	0.97031912	1.351	0.1817	1.2970854
Income	1	0.786267	0.45160971	1.741	0.0866	1.3638940
Duration of Care	1	0.762568	0.54676118	1.395	0.1681	1.0480170
Elder Health Status	1	-0.455500	0.48553298	-0.938	0.3518	1.2631707
Elder Mental Status	1	-0.121776	0.11811008	-1.031	0.3065	1.1374789
Level of Willingness	1	-1.436896	1.21237602	-1.185	0.2405	1.0708864

TABLE 11

MULTIPLE REGRESSION OF THE RELATIONSHIP BETWEEN THE LEVEL OF WILLINGNESS
AND CAREGIVER STRAIN (REDUCED VARIABLE MODEL)

Analysis of Variance

Source	DF	Sum of Squares	Mean Square	F Value	Prob>F	Adjusted R square
Model	6	96.686	16.114	1.232	0.3019	0.0195
Error	64	837.145	13.080			
C Total	70	933.831				

Parameter Estimates

Variable	DF	Parameter Estimate	Standard Error	T for HO: Parameter = 0	Prob >|T|	Variance Inflation
Intercept	1	10.624691	3.45174953	3.078	0.0031	0.0000000
Race	1	-0.223294	1.04808276	-0.213	0.8320	1.2419420
Proximity	1	1.705399	0.95884681	1.779	0.0801	1.2354748
Income	1	0.488601	0.42224832	1.157	0.2515	1.1630168
Elder Health Status	1	-0.500707	0.48924076	-1.023	0.3100	1.2510248
Elder Mental Status	1	-0.094607	0.11862425	-0.798	0.4281	1.1192121
Level of Willing ness	1	-1.175554	1.21772110	-0.965	0.3380	1.0538055

Multivariate Analysis of Relationship Between Reason for Selection and Caregiver Strain

A general linear models procedure was performed to multivariately test the relationship between the reason for selection into the caregiving role and the level of caregiver strain. The relationship between the dependent variable, caregiver strain, and the independent variable, reason for selection, was tested while controlling for caregiver race, residential proximity, marital status, household income, duration of caregiving and elder factors (physical health status and mental status).

Results appear in Table 12. Again, no variables in this model are statistically significant at the .05 level. However, the independent variable, reason for selection which was entered as a categorical variable, has marginal statistical significance (p<0.0842) as do two of the control variables, caregiver residential proximity (p<0.0868) and caregiver household income (p<0.0907). The adjusted R-square is .0751.

Regression Diagnostic Analysis. Multicollinearity was checked using Fox's guidelines (Fox, 1991) in evaluating the variance inflation factors. This inspection indicated no problem with multicollinearity.

Additional Exploratory Analysis. The fact that caregiver reason for selection, were marginally significant warranted further examination. Therefore, three additional regression procedures were performed using part or all of the variables in this exploration.

TABLE 12
MULTIVARIATE ANALYSIS OF RELATIONSHIP BETWEEN
CAREGIVER REASON FOR SELECTION AND CAREGIVER STRAIN

General Linear Models Procedure

Source	DF	Sum of Squares	Mean Square	F Value	Prob>F	Adjusted R square
Model	10	205.817	20.582	1.70	0.1026	0.0751
Error	60	728.014	12.134			
C Total	70	933.831				

Source	DF	Type III SS	Mean Square	F Value	Prob > F
Race	1	1.4081288	1.4081288	0.12	0.7345
Proximity	1	43.6533014	43.6533014	3.60	0.0627
Marital Status	1	3.0902740	3.0902740	0.25	0.6156
Income	1	35.8614006	35.8614006	2.96	0.0907
Duration of Care	1	23.6661436	23.6661436	1.95	0.1677
Elder Health Status	1	4.6213178	4.6213178	0.38	0.5395
Elder Mental Status	1	12.5497907	12.5497907	1.03	0.3132
Reason for Selection	3	80.9666403	26.9888801	2.22	0.0946

A "leaps and bounds" regression procedure (used to identify the combination of independent variables with the most predictive power) and a general linear models procedure (with a reduced number of variables) were performed. The first, regression by "leaps and bounds" procedure, indicated the best model to be a four-variable model which included: caregiver residential proximity; elder physical health status; elder mental status and the reason for selection category, family structure and duty/obligation. The R-square for this model was 0.15; F value was 3.01 (p<0.02). Caregiver residential proximity and the reason for selection category, family structure and duty/obligation, both reached statistical significance at the .05 level in this model. Findings are presented in Table 13.

The second procedure, a reduced variable general linear models procedure, included the same five control variables as described in the willingness model: race, caregiver residential proximity, caregiver household income; elder physical health status and elder mental status. The findings are presented in Table 14. The R-square for this procedure is 0.18 with the independent variable, reason for selection, reaching marginal statistical significance (p<.0648).

This procedure was repeated, deleting caregiver household income. The findings are presented in Table 15. The R-square in this reduced variable model is 0.17 with the independent variable, reason for selection emerging as statistically significant (p<0.0516).

Analysis was performed to determine the presence of interactions between the independent variables in regard to the dependent variable, caregiver strain. No evidence of interactions was noted.

Post-hoc Testing. Post-hoc means tests were performed using the Duncan Multiple Range Test which indicated that Category 3—family structure and duty/obligation is significantly different from the Category 4—self-decision. These findings, presented in Table 16, suggest that daughter caregivers who assume the caregiving role for reasons related to their sense of duty and obligation to the parent report that they experience higher levels of strain than daughters who decide for themselves to assume the caregiving role.

TABLE 13

MULTIVARIATE ANALYSIS OF RELATIONSHIP BETWEEN CAREGIVER REASON FOR SELECTION AND CAREGIVER STRAIN (LEAPS AND BOUNDS PROCEDURE)

Maximum R-square Improvement for Dependent Variable, Caregiver Strain

	DF	Sum of Squares	Mean Square	F Value	Prob>F	R-Square
Regression	4	144.0748257	36.0187064	3.01	0.0242	0.154284
Error	66	789.7561603	11.9660024			
Total	70	933.8309859				

Variable	Parameter Estimate	Standard Error	Type II SS	F Value	Prob>F
Intercept	9.629966	1.763927	356.645494	29.80	0.0001
Proximity	1.759674	0.890874	46.685339	3.90	0.0524
Elder Health Status	-0.607533	0.456010	221.239329	1.77	0.1873
Elder Mental Status	-0.132508	0.113820	16.217718	1.36	0.2485
Reason for Selection (Duty)	2.931870	1.077449	88.602362	7.40	0.0083

Bounds on condition number: 1.188065, 18.04222   The above model is the best 4-variable model found.

TABLE 14
MULTIVARIATE ANALYSIS OF RELATIONSHIP BETWEEN
CAREGIVER REASON FOR SELECTION
AND CAREGIVER STRAIN (Five control variables)

General Linear Models Procedure

Source	DF	Sum of Squares	Mean Square	F Value	Prob>F
Model	8	168.267	21.033	1.70	0.1154
Error	62	765.564	12.347		
C Total	70	933.831			

Source	DF	Type III SS	Mean Square	F Value	Prob > F
Race	1	1.0698483	1.0698483	0.09	0.7695
Proximity	1	40.9400749	40.9400749	3.32	0.0735
Income	1	7.7715973	7.7715973	0.63	0.4306
Elder Health Status	1	16.4534140	16.4534140	1.33	0.2528
Elder Mental Status	1	18.0735024	18.0735024	1.46	0.2309
Reason for Selection	3	83.7716311	27.9238770	2.26	0.0901

TABLE 15

MULTIVARIATE ANALYSIS OF RELATIONSHIP BETWEEN
CAREGIVER REASON FOR SELECTION
AND CAREGIVER STRAIN (Four control variables)

General Linear Models Procedure

Source	DF	Sum of Squares	Mean Square	F Value	Prob>F
Model	7	160.496	22.928	1.87	0.0899
Error	63	773.335	12.275		
C Total	70	933.831			

Source	DF	Type III SS	Mean Square	F Value	Prob>F
Race	1	3.9212751	3.9212751	0.32	0.5739
Proximity	1	43.9836238	43.9836238	3.58	0.0630
Elder Health Status	1	18.1388163	18.1388163	1.48	0.2287
Elder Mental Status	1	16.9304076	16.9304076	1.38	0.2447
Reason for Selection	3	100.332284	33.4440946	2.72	0.0516

TABLE 16

COMPARISON OF MEAN STRAIN LEVEL BY
REASON FOR SELECTION CATEGORY

Caregiver Strain

Reason for Selection Category	Group Means	Duncan Multiple Range Test[1]	
CATEGORY 1:			
Request	7.94	A	B
CATEGORY 2:			
No Alternative	8.03	A	B
CATEGORY 3:			
Family Structure and Duty/Obligation	10.31	A	
CATEGORY 4:			
Self-Decision	6.75		B

* p<.05

[1]Means with the same letter are not significantly different

V
Discussion

INTRODUCTION

The aim of this study was to build on existing knowledge regarding caregiver strain experienced by daughters who serve as the primary caregiver for an elderly parent. Specifically, an examination was conducted to determine if relationships exist between caregiver strain and two caregiver induction factors, caregiver level of willingness to assume the caregiving role and the reason the caregiver was selected into the role. Seven variables were conceptualized as control variables in the analysis because empirical evidence links these factors to caregiver strain. These variables relate to the caregiver and the elder and include: caregiver race, marital status, duration of caregiving, caregiver annual household income and physical proximity to the elder and elder physical health status and mental status.

Two research questions were developed for the study:

1. Is the level of willingness to assume the caregiving role associated with caregiver strain?
2. Does caregiver strain differ according to the reason for selection?

The sample for this study included seventy daughters who serve as the primary caregiver for an elderly, community-dwelling parent. The data were collected from three ongoing research projects. The studies include: *Adequacy of Home Care for Chronically Ill Elderly* (CPS) (Proctor, Morrow-Howell and Chadiha 1990), *Increasing the Awareness of Alzheimer's Disease and Unmet Needs and Strengths of African-American Caregivers of Elderly Alzheimer's Patients* (Chadiha andd Morrow-Howell 1991) and *Memory and Aging Project Satellite* (MAPS) (Berg and Edwards 1993). Telephone interviews were conducted with fifty-two daughter caregivers in the Care Plan Study and Memory and Aging Project samples. Face-to-face interviews had previously been conducted with nineteen daughter caregivers from the African-American study and the data were incorporated into the analysis. The relationships of the independent variables and the dependent variable were examined through the use of multivariate analysis. Prior to multivariate analysis of the second research question, five categories were developed through content analysis for the reason for selection variable. The categories were then reduced to four for conceptual and empirical reasons. Findings will be further discussed in this chapter.

DISCUSSION OF FINDINGS

The multivariate relationships between the independent variables and the dependent variable, caregiver strain, as identified in the two research questions will be discussed. Contributions of this research to the knowledge base regarding caregiver strain among daughter caregivers will be highlighted.

Level of Willingness to Assume the Caregiving Role

Multivariately, no relationship was found between the caregiver's self-reported level of willingness to assume the caregiving role and caregiver-perceived strain. As described in the previous chapter, the model was further analyzed using two procedures, multiple regression by leaps and bounds and multiple regression with a reduced number of variables. Level of willingness still did not emerge as statistically significant in these analyses.

Caregiver proximity to the elder reached marginal statistical significance with caregiver strain in the analyses. This variable was measured dichotomously by caregiver co-residence or non-co-residence with the elder. In the initial multiple regression analysis, the F value for caregiver proximity to the elder was 1.70 ($p<0.0939$). In the best model developed through the leaps and bounds procedure, the F value was 3.49 ($p<0.0663$); in the reduced variable multiple regression procedure, the F value was 1.889 ($p<0.0634$).

The finding which suggests caregiver proximity to the elder is related to caregiver strain is consistent with the literature. First, the literature on the role of physical proximity in caregiving suggests proximity is related to the caregiver's assumption of the role (Horowitz 1985b; Lang and Brody 1983; and Older Women's League 1989). Specifically, proximity has been linked to willingness and ability to provide care (Kivett and Anderson 1984) and familial obligation (Finley, et al. 1988). Secondly, residential proximity has been linked with caregiver strain through increased caregiving task intensity (Biegel, et al. 1991; Eagles, et al. 1987; and Reece, et al. 1983). However, the literature was somewhat conflicted regarding the role of proximity in determining caregiver strain. Several studies (Pearson, et al. 1988; Staight and Harvey 1990; and Stoller and Pugliesi 1989a) suggest co-residing with the elder can result in decreased caregiver strain levels as caregivers are able to focus on caregiving to the exclusion of other responsibilities which lessens the perceived burden. This provides support for proximity as a factor related to caregiver strain. This finding further provides support for an earlier report that physical closeness to the elder may provide increased opportunities for caregiving (Lee 1980). Closer proximity may then result in increased caregiver strain which also supports earlier findings which indicate caregiver selection is often linked to physical proximity (Older Women's League 1989). Specifically, physical proximity may impact the amount of care provided which suggests that increased caregiving provided results in increased caregiver strain. This further raises the possibility that increased physical distance results in less caregiving provided and, ultimately, less caregiving strain.

A second control variable, caregiver household income, was also marginally statistically significant; therefore, the variable was retained for further exploratory analysis. However, this variable did not approach statistical significance in further analyses.

As noted, there was no statistically significant relationship found between caregiver level of willingness to assume the role and caregiver strain. There are three potential explanations for these lack of findings. First, there may actually be no relationship between caregiver level of willingness to assume the role and caregiver strain. While the literature suggests willingness to assume the role is related to caregiver strain, the lack of empirical study of the area and development of a standardized measure has left the question unexplored for the most part. The possibility that no actual relationship exists between caregiver level of willingness to assume the role and caregiver strain suggests that other factors may have greater impact on caregiver strain than willingness to assume the role.

Secondly, the way in which the caregiver's level of willingness to assume the role was measured may be an inaccurate depiction of the caregiver's true experience. A one-item measure may not fully capture the caregiver's feelings as the measure may have been too simplistic. Moreover, the wording of this item may have promoted socially desirable responses. The issue of the measure and the potential for eliciting social desirable responses will be further discussed in the section on limitations of the study.

Lastly, a methodological problem may exist. Despite power analysis that indicates an 72% chance of detecting a real relationship, there remains a 28% chance of a Type II error occurring where an actual relationship fails to be identified. An increase in sample size will increase the power and the ability to detect a true relationship.

Caregiver Reason for Selection

An outcome from this analysis is the development of categories to identify reason caregivers are selected into the caregiving role. As noted, few researchers have previously conducted formal explorations of this issue. Guberman and colleagues (1992) identified fourteen categories—six primary and eight secondary categories—which determine caregiver selection. Reasons for selection were organized into three cluster groups: 1) factors related to the caregiver's material, social and psychological status—love, need to help, duty, socioeconomic dependence, anti-institutional feelings, caregiving arrangement, religious feelings, personal characteristics, belief in healing and family tradition; 2) factors related to the availability of resources—inadequate/unavailable family, community and institutional resources; and 3) factors related to the care-receiver—imposition and health. Guberman and colleagues suggest the reason caregivers are selected are a result of multiple factors which interrelate. Albert (1990) suggests caregivers assume the caregiving role for reasons related to repayment of a parental debt, sense of obligation to provide care and lack of caregiving resources.

Using the categories developed by these previous research efforts for comparison, several similarities are noted. Five categories were identified from the content analysis conducted in this study: 1)

Request, 2) No other alternative or resource, 3) Family position/structure, 4) Duty and/or obligation to provide care and 5) Self-decision to provide care. The third and fourth categories were combined for analysis for conceptual and empirical reasons. Similarities can be noted in Table 17.

In performing multivariate analysis with the variable, reason for caregiver selection, and the dependent variable, caregiver strain, no statistically significant relationship was found. The relationship of the independent variable, reason for caregiver selection, and two control variables, caregiver physical proximity to the elder and caregiver household income, to caregiver strain was marginally significant in the initial analysis. The F value for caregiver reason for selection was 2.32 ($p<0.0842$), while the F value for caregiver proximity was 3.03 ($p<0.0868$) and the F value for caregiver household income was 2.96 ($p<0.0907$). Furthermore, when additional exploratory analyses were conducted through the leaps and bounds procedure and a reduced variable multiple regression procedure, only two of these variables emerged at or near statistically significant levels ($p<0.05$). Caregiver household income did not approach statistical significance in any of the further exploratory analyses. In the leaps and bounds procedure, the F value for proximity was 3.58 ($p<0.0630$). Three categories of reason for selection were dummy coded with the category related to family position/structure and duty/obligation having an F value of 7.24 ($p<0.0091$). In the reduced variable general linear models procedure, the F value for reason for selection was 2.72 ($p<0.0516$). While marginal, these findings suggest that the reason the caregiver was selected into the role may be related to the strain perceived by the caregiver.

TABLE 17

REASONS FOR SELECTION BY STUDY

Guberman (1991)	Albert (1990)	Berg-Weger (1993)
Imposition (by elder)	Repayment of debt	Request
Inadequate or unavailable resources	Unavailability of caregiver	No other alternative or resource
Family tradition		Family position or structure
Duty	Caregiver is responsible to provide care	Duty or obligation
Need to help		Self-decision to provide care

These similarities provide evidence to suggest that it is possible to identify categories for reasons for selection. Replication of this exploration may provide evidence to further delineate these categories and link them to caregiving outcomes.

One control variable, caregiver physical proximity to the elder, emerged consistently throughout the analyses as a marginally significant factor related to caregiver strain. Specifically, co-resident caregivers reported high levels of caregiver strain. While elders and caregivers are in agreement that close proximity is not essential for caregiver selection (Hamon 1988; Hamon and Blieszner 1990; Hanson, et al. 1983), this study provides support for the two factors being related. Furthermore, others report that proximity may, in fact, be related to the caregiver's sense of familial obligation to provide care, suggesting that decreased proximity fosters less obligation to provide care (Finley, et al. 1988).

As noted, the relationship between the independent variable and one control variable, caregiver physical proximity to the elder, with caregiver strain reached marginal statistical significance. These findings, while not statistically significant at the 0.05 probability level, warranted further exploratory analysis. The additional exploratory analysis produced results within a range to permit further post hoc testing. The post hoc means tests indicated that caregivers who assume the role for reasons related to family position/structure or out of a sense of duty or obligation to the elder perceive higher levels of strain than caregivers who assume the role based on a self-decision to do so. Caregivers in the higher strain groups may perceive a stronger sense of filial duty to provide care to an elderly parent. The caregiver may feel caregiving is an obligation mandated by an expectation from the family, an expectation based on the caregiver's position in the family, family "rules" regarding caregiving responsibilities or a self-imposed responsibility to provide care. In sum, daughter caregivers who report selection is due to one of these reasons may feel she is fated to become a caregiver and that she has little or no control over the eventual outcome of that decision. Whereas, daughter caregivers who decide for themselves to assume the caregiving role may feel a greater sense of control over the decision, thus evoking more positive feelings about caregiving in general.

While Guberman and colleagues (1991) and Albert (1990) did not examine reason for selection in relation to an outcome as in this study, both report that caregiver factors are strong determinants of caregiver identity. This supposition can be related to the findings of this study. Specifically, assuming a caregiving role for reasons related to family structure or position in the family or a sense of duty and obligation are reasons which relate directly to the caregiver as an individual, separate from the elder, the caregiver's family or the caregiving situation or arrangement. This provides further support for the identification of the reason for selection categories and a possible link to caregiver strain.

Non-significance of Control Variables. The variables included in this analysis as control variables were selected as the literature suggested an empirical relationship with caregiver strain. Of note is the fact that no statistically significant relationships were found between any of the other six control variables (caregiver race, marital status, household income and duration of caregiving and elder physical health status and mental status) and caregiver strain. Additionally, there was no statistically significant relationship found between the sample source and caregiver strain.

While the data from this study cannot provide an explanation for the lack of significant relationships being detected between these variables and caregiver strain, the literature may, again, provide insight. For example, the literature does suggest that differences exist in the role strain of African-American and White daughter caregiver (Mui 1992). In the case of the effect of race on the caregiving experience, the real influence of race on caregiving may be family and ethnic culture rather than race itself. Mui (1992) suggests such family and cultural factors as filial obligation, relationship quality and work conflicts impact the caregiver's experience of strain. As no relationship was detected between race and caregiver strain in this study, the need for further examination of the experience of caregiving by different racial groups is suggested.

Secondly, caregiver marital status has been linked to caregiver strain. The literature suggests that younger caregivers (who are more likely to be married) experience high levels of strain. However, married caregivers may have more social support available to them which serves as a buffer against the strain of caregiving (Brody, et al. 1992). Caregiver financial status may also be related to lower caregiver strain. Daughter caregivers from higher socioeconomic status levels are known to have the capability to purchase care which can lessen the strain experienced (Archbold 1983). Married daughter caregivers may fall into this category as well and perceive less strain due to their ability to purchase/share care. The findings presented in this study support the idea that marital status and caregiver income do not impact caregiver strain. While the literature is conflicted on the relationship between caregiver marital status and income and strain, this study provides support for the research that suggests marital status and income are not related to caregiver strain.

Finally, elder physical health status and mental status have both been linked to caregiver strain. The findings are conflicted regarding the impact of the phase of the elder's illness which can relate to the duration of caregiving. While this study does not provide support for these relationships, the findings do raise questions regarding the relationships and warrant further examination.

LIMITATIONS OF THE STUDY

Three limitations to this study can be noted. The three areas to be discussed here include: 1) Sample size, 2) Caregiver strain measure and 3) Willingness to assume the caregiving role measure.

Sample Size

First, the sample size may have been too small to enable the detection of statistically significant findings for the two research questions. A larger sample size may have increased the power of the analysis and, subsequently, resulted in the identification of statistically significant findings. Replication of this study with a larger sample may be warranted.

Caregiver Strain Measure

Secondly, the scale used to measure the dependent variable, caregiver strain, may have limited the range of caregiver responses regarding the perceived strain experienced in caregiving. This limitation may have resulted in the study's inability to fully capture the respondent's caregiving experience. Specifically, this instrument was not validated on a cross-section of caregivers of elders with diverse health conditions. The scale was validated on caregivers of elders with arteriosclerotic heart disease or post-hip surgery only (Robinson 1983). Furthermore, this scale was initially designed for use in identifying potential hospital discharge care plan problems and may be more useful as a screening tool for caregiver strain rather than a validation of such a condition. Because the instrument has not been validated with other populations of caregivers, its validity for the daughter caregivers in this study may be in question. For future study, an instrument which measures the caregiver's response to caregiving over time may be a more accurate method for capturing the experience. A cross-sectional view of this phenomena is limiting.

Willingness to Assume the Caregiving Role Measure

A final limitation of this study may be the method used to measure the caregiver's level of willingness to assume the caregiving role. This variable was measured by a one-item Likert-type scale developed for the African-American caregiver study (Chadiha and Morrow-Howell 1991). While the item includes five categories which allows the caregiver to select from a range of responses, the content of the question may have prompted the respondent to provide a response she perceived to be socially desirable. For replication, this variable may better be measured through the use of a series of items developed to capture the subtleties of caregiver willingness. The caregiver may have felt forced into providing a positive answer to such a direct, one-item question regarding the care of her parent.

Secondly, the problem of defining the meaning of "willingness" is inherent in a one-item measure. Specifically, the concept of willingness to provide care to a elderly, frail parent may have different meaning to different persons. Caregivers who had been providing care for some period of time were asked to retrospectively recall their level of willingness to assume the role at the time of induction. The respondents may not have been able to convey an accurate depiction of willingness if they had attempted to make other arrangements for the parent and had to provide care because they perceived no other alternative to exist.

IMPLICATIONS OF RESEARCH

Implications of this research emerge in three areas: theory, practice and future research. Implications in each of these areas will be discussed.

Implications for Theory

The research questions were driven by two theories. First, role theory was used to establish caregiving as a role, define the tasks performed within the caregiving experience and offer insight into the relationship between role induction and caregiver strain. Secondly, social exchange theory was extended to explain the relationships between the reasons for caregiving selection and caregiver strain.

In regard to role theory, the data suggest that caregivers view caregiving as a role to be assumed. This is evidenced by the reasons for selection identified by the caregivers. Specifically, some caregivers in this study perceive the role to be imposed upon them by others—a concept suggested by Goode (1960). Doty's (1986) work, which suggested that caregivers perceive caregiving to be more important than other responsibilities, is supported here by the fact some caregivers assume the role out of a sense of duty and obligation.

This theory was also used to suggest that caregiver willingness to assume the role is a result of internal or external gratification (Goode 1960). While the group of daughters studied did report an overall high level of willingness to assume the caregiving role, no relationship was established between level of willingness to assume the role and caregiver strain. While specifically tested in this study, a possible explanation may be that caregivers who report a high level of willingness to assume the role are also experiencing a high level of internal or external gratification which was not captured by the willingness measure. However, as noted the small sample size and/or the willingness measure itself may have prevented the detection of such a relationship.

To further develop the understanding of the relationship between role theory and caregiver experiences, additional research is needed. "A multiple roles perspective is needed to broaden understanding of the stressfulness of the elder care role" (Choi 1993). Specifically, further examination of the sociodemographic and qualitative variables related to the caregiver role is warranted. As noted by Mui (1995), an qualitative exploration is necessary to delve into the contributions of such variables as role demand overloads, conflict, expectations, adequacy, satisfaction and preparedness for caregiving. Spitze and colleagues (1994) additionally suggest further research to identify the ways in which adult child caregivers make decisions to provide care and the methods used for providing efficient care in light of multiple, competing roles.

Social exchange theory was used to derive the second research question and provide an explanation for reasons for caregiver selection into the caregiving role and the strain experienced within the role. Specifically, the theory was used to establish a connection between such reasons for selection as love and feelings of family ties, feelings of duty and obligation, elder request and family tradition (reasons cited in Guberman et al., 1991). While the theory had not been empirically tested using these reasons, it suggests that reasons for selection which relate to social exchange factors (repayment of a debt or purchase of future "credit") result in a different level of caregiver strain. The findings do suggest, however, that caregivers who assume the caregiving role for reasons related to a sense of duty and obligation or family position experience higher levels of caregiver strain. The literature on social exchange theory suggests that caregivers who provide care out of a need to repay a parental debt or reciprocate would be less strained. However, this study suggests the opposite actually occurs. Further, there appears to be a trend in the data to suggest that caregivers who decide for themselves to assume the caregiving role are the least stressed. As noted by Chesla and colleagues (1994, p 8–9), caregiving may be ". . . the genuine working out and fulfillment of a lifelong relationship; therefore, it is not experienced as burdensome, but sustaining and meaningful." While this study is not a test of social exchange theory, it is an attempt to explain caregiver strain using a social exchange theory perspective.

While two theoretical perspectives frequently used to explain caregiver strain, role and social exchange theories, motivated the development of the research questions, it should be noted that other less commonly used theoretical perspectives may also serve to provide insight into caregiver strain. First, attribution theory (Heider 1958), derived from a social psychological perspective, provides a framework for explaining the reasons people choose to behave in certain ways and the consequences associated with the reasons. Causality is determined and decisions are made when information which is taken in covaries with the individual's prior beliefs (Kelley 1973). This theory may aid in explaining the relationship between caregiver role induction and strain by viewing the reasons caregivers are selected in terms of "process" (the way beliefs are explained), "content" (the way individuals categorize explanations) and "consequents" (behavioral outcomes of explanations) (Lewis and Daltroy 1990). Caregivers who perceive themselves to be experiencing high levels of strain may have a negative perception regarding the role induction process. Using Kelley's (1973) discounting principle (cause will be discounted if other causes are possible), it may be possible that caregivers who evaluate the caregiving situation as strained will attribute that effect to the situation (tasks) itself and not his or her level of willingness or decision to assume the role. Further, Kelley (1973) suggests individuals attribute an effect to internal and external causes which may covary. This can imply that caregivers with a positive attitude toward the caregiving induction process may perceive a more positve effect resulting in a lower perceived strain level. Attribution theory has been used to explore the relationship between caregiver-elder co-residence and caregiver risk for depression (Cohen and Eisdorfer 1988). The findings suggest that co-resident caregivers who perceived a loss of control over their environment and attributed this to an internal cause were at a higher risk for depression. This theory may be used to explore the relationship of the role played by the caregiver's attributions about caregiving and the outcome of caregiving for the caregiver (in this case, the outcome is strain).

A second theoretical perspective which may prove fruitful as an explanation for the relationship between caregiver role induction and caregiver strain is the theory of the provisions of social relationships (Weiss 1974). The theory of social provisions seeks to explain the reasons why individuals seek out and sustain relationships with others. Weiss maintains that different relationships provide individuals with different provisions and a balance/mixture of provisions are needed at different developmental stages to maintain an individual's sense well-being and prevent distress. Weiss (1974, 22) presents six categories of relational provisions: 1) "Attachment"—the individual gains a sense of security, usually from a spouse/partner; 2) "Social Integration"—the individual gains companionship and/or an exchange of services, typically provided by friends; 3) "Opportunity for Nurturance"—the individual develops a sense of being needed, often provided by kin; 4) "Reassurance of Worth"—the individual gains a sense of role competence (can be provided by co-workers/friends); 5) "Reliable Alliance"—Typically provided by kin, the individual is assured of continued assistance despite the presence of affection or reciprocation; and 6) "Guidance"—the individual is the recipient of mentoring from a teacher or friend. Without the appropriate balance of these provisions, an individual may experience distress in the form of social/emotional isolation, meaninglessness, low self-esteem, vulnerability and/or anxiety (Weiss, 1974). While not used to explore the relationship between caregiver role induction and caregiver strain, this theory has been used to explain perceptions of social support by elders and new parents (Cutrano 1986). Cutrano reports that not only do relationships provide certain provisions (as suggested by Weiss 1974), but that kin relationships are more effective than non-kin relationships in providing provisions.

In sum, this discussion suggests that the implications for the application of theory to the phenomena of caregiver role induction and its effects have only just begun to be explored. Two theories, role and social exchange theories, were used in this study to suggest an explanation for the relationship between caregiver role induction and strain; however, it is evident that other theories may be relevant for use in further exploration.

Implications for Social Work Practice

The data do indicate that this group of daughter caregivers were experiencing moderately high levels of strain. This suggests caregiver interventions may be more effective if targeted at other areas related to caregiving. Specifically, interventions can be targeted at areas of caregiving in which caregivers perceive they have the greatest needs. Since caregiver proximity to the elder consistently emerged as a factor related to caregiver strain, interventions which focus on the provision of respite care may be more effective than interventions directed at aiding families in identifying a caregiver. Further, recent research has shown that enabling caregivers to engage in enjoyable, social activities may serve to reduce the burden associated with caregiving (Thompson, Futterman, Gallagher-Thompson, Rose and Lovett 1993).

The information gained here can be used to design interventions in other areas, particularly for caregivers identified as assuming the role for reasons related to their sense of duty and/or obligation. Since this group appears to experience higher levels of stress than other groups of caregivers, further exploration of their caregiving experience may be warranted. This research supports the recommendations of other researchers (Chesla, et al. 1994) regarding the merit of early, educational interventions which may enable family members to anticipate and prepare for the caregiving role. Interventions may be designed which build on the evidence on both ends of the continuum. For both those caregivers who self-select into the role and are founds to experience less caregiver strain and those who are provide care out of a sense of duty or obligation, interventions which target the positive aspects of reciprocity and past care-recipient contributions may enable the caregiver to reframe the experience in a more positive light (Walker, Pratt and Oppy 1992). For those caregivers experiencing only low to moderate levels of strain, interventions focussing on stress/strain prevention, information and support may merit further exploration (Walker, et al. 1995).

Finally, in examining the future of family caregiving, several factors should be considered in planning and implementing caregiver interventions. As family resources (number and availability of adult children) decreases, it will be the gender make-up of the family grouping (versus the actual number of children) that will determine parent care arrangements (Montgomery 1992). Further, while adult daughters will continue to serve as primary caregivers of elder parents, more care will be purchased due to the increasing numbers of women who are employed outside the home (Montgomery 1992). This evidence suggests that practitioners may aid family caregivers in re-conceptualizing their sense of filial obligation and the manner in which care will be provided to the elderly parents (Montgomery 1992).

Implications for Future Research

The findings from this study can be used to suggest: 1) there is a need to replicate the study with a larger sample over a period of time; 2) the caregiver's level of willingness to assume the caregiving role may be more accurately measured by a stronger, more reliable method of measurement, one that will account for the social desirability factor; and 3) replication is needed to strengthen the reason for caregiver selection categories. Further work is needed on measurement approaches of this factor to address such issues as consistency and biases which may occur with self-reported perceptions.

As noted by Dwyer and Coward (Coward and Dwyer 1992), future caregiving research may benefit from a shift in focus which will include cross-cultural and family (versus dyadic) samples, interdisciplinary collaboration efforts and tools which will distinguish between related factors (gender, age, cohorts and health status). Consistent with Dwyer and Coward's recommendations regarding the need for examining caregiving within a cultural context, Morrison (1995) calls for the development of a research agenda to include exploration into the needs of family caregivers, particularly within a racial, ethnic, socioeconomic realm, and the implications of those needs for policy and program development.

Additionally, further study of the caregiver reason for selection categories derived from this study may warranted. The two caregiver reason for selection categories—family structure/duty and obligation and self-decision—which were shown to be different may represent the opposite ends of a continuum of caregiver reasons for selection. These categories may reflect the extent to which the caregiver reason for selection is related to the caregiver's free choosing to assume the caregiving role. Specifically, the the mean strain level by reason for selection category were ordered from high to low as: 1) family structure/duty and obligation (10. 31); 2) no alternative (8.03); 3) request (7.94); and 4) self-decision (6.75). This may suggest, for example, that caregivers who assume the caregiving role for reasons related to family structure/duty and obligation (highest strain level) perceive the least amount of free choice, while caregivers who decide for themselves they want to assume the role (lowest strain level) may perceive they have the most free choice.

The development of a new measurement tool to measure the caregiver's reason for selection on a freedom of choice continuum may aid in furthering our understanding of the caregiver role induction experience. As noted by Montgomery (1992, 81), ". . . this care is to be provided is simply a sense of self-imposed obligation about which little is known, but that remains persistent." Such future research may address the issue raised by Montgomery regarding self-imposed obligation and build, as well, on the work of Loomis and Booth (1995) who have explored multigenerational caregiving. Specifically, the research of Loomis and Booth (1995) suggests that caregivers self-select into a role such as caregiving because they are able to competently balance multiple roles (parent and child care, for instance). Loomis and Booth further suggest that multiple role demands are not experienced negatively by the caregiver as all care-recipients are known to the caregiver, the caregiver may have a strong marital relationship and caregiving is valued. The development of a "freedom of choice" measure may deepen the understanding of reasons some caregivers appear to assume more responsibilities that are feasible.

SUMMARY

The aim of this study to contribute to the existing knowledge base regarding caregiving strain has been achieved. Adult daughter caregivers of elderly parents who were interviewed provided insight into the experience of caregiving which support the following:

1. Level of willingness to assume the caregiving role is not related to caregiver strain
2. Caregivers who assume the role for reasons related to family structure and/or a sense of duty and obligation experience a higher level of caregiver strain than caregivers who decide for themselves to assume the role and
3. Caregiver physical proximity to the elder may be related to the caregiver's perceived level of strain.

Despite the weaknesses of this research which have been discussed, three themes emerged which suggest the need for further investigation. First, this work is the first attempt to empirically study the area of caregiver role induction. Secondly, despite the fact that caregiver level of willingness to assume the caregiving role was not related to caregiver strain, this was an initial attempt to examine this aspect of caregiving. The development of a more accurate measure of this variable may yield additional information as well. Finally, categories were developed which identified reasons for caregiver selection into the caregiving role. Further exploration through replication may yield fruitful information to be used in gaining insight into the outcome of caregiving for the caregiver.

In sum, by examining the relationship between two caregiver induction factors and strain, this study provides the basis for future examination of this relatively unexplored area of family caregiving. The direction of future research can focus on further delineating the measures used in this study and beginning to examine the impact of caregiver role induction on other caregiving outcomes.

Bibliography

Albert, S. M. 1990. Caregiving as a cultural system: Conceptions of filial obligation and parental dependency in urban America. *American Anthropologist*, 92:319–330.

Aldous, J. 1994. Someone to watch over me. Family responsibilities and their realization across family lives. In *Family caregiving across the lifespan*, eds. E. Kahana, D.E. Biegel, and M.L. Wykle, 42–68. Thousand Oaks, California: Sage Publications.

American Association of Retired Persons and Administration on Aging. 1992. *Profile of older Americans*. Washington, D.C.: U.S. Department of Health and Human Services.

Anastas, J. W., J. L. Gibeau, and P. J. Larson. 1990. Working families and eldercare: A national perspective in an aging America. *Social Work*, 35(5):405–411.

Anthony-Bergstone, C. R., S. H. Zarit and M. Gatz. 1988. Symptoms of psychological distress among caregivers of demented patients. *Psychology and Aging*, 3(3):245–248.

Archbold, P. G. 1983. Impact of parent-caring on women. *Family Relations*, 32:39–45.

Bailey, K. D. 1978. *Methods of social research*. New York: The Free Press.

Baillie, V., J. S. Norbeck and L. E. Barnes. 1988. Stress, social support and psychological distress of family caregivers of the elderly. *Nursing Research*, 37(4): 217–222.

Barnett, R. C. and G. K. Baruch. 1985. Women's involvement in multiple roles and psychological distress. *Journal of Personality and Social Psychology*, 49(1):135–145.

Baruch, G. K. and R. Barnett. 1986. Role quality, multiple role involvement, and psychological well-being in mid-life women. *Journal of Personality and Social Psychology*, 51:578–585.

Barusch, A. S. 1988. Problems and coping strategies of elderly spouse caregivers. *The Gerontologist*, 28(5):677–685.

Barusch, A .S. and W. M. Spaid. 1989. Gender differences in caregiving: Why do wives report greater burden? *The Gerontologist*, 29(5):667–676.

Berg, L. and D. Edwards. 1993. *Memory and Aging Project Satellite*. Alzheimer's Disease Research Center, Washington University School of Medicine. Grant funded by the National Institute on Aging.

Berg-Weger, M. and D. M. Rubio. 1996. Role induction and caregiver strain: A structural equation approach. *Journal of Social Service Research*. In press.

Biegel, D. E., E. Sales and R. Schulz. 1991. *Family caregiving in chronic illness*. Newbury Park, California: Sage Publications.

Blessed, G., B. E. Tomlinson and M. Roth. 1968. The association between quantitative measures of dementia and of senile change in the cerebral grey matter of elderly subjects. *British Journal of Psychiatry, 114:*797–811.

Blieszner, R. and R. R. Hamon. 1992. Filial responsibility: Attitudes, motivators and behaviors. In *Gender, families and elder care*, eds. J. W. Dwyer and R. T. Coward, 105–119. Newbury Park, California: Sage Publications.

Blieszner, R. and J. A. Mancini. 1987. Enduring ties: Older adults' parental role and responsibilities. *Family Relations, 36:*176–180.

Borenstein, M. and J. Cohen. 1988. Statistical Power Analysis Computer Program.

Braithwaite, V. 1986. The burden of home care: How is it shared? *Supplement to Community Health Studies X,* 3:7.s–11.s.

Brittain, L. and M. Dellmann-Jenkins. 1995. Young adults' perceptions of filial responsibility: An exploratory study. Poster presentation at National Council on Family Relations, Portland, Oregon.

Brody, E. M. 1981. "Women in the middle" and family help to older people. *TheGerontologist,* 21(5):471–480.

———, 1985a. Filial care of the elderly and changing roles of women (and men). Paper presented at the 25th Anniversary Scientific Meeting of the Boston Society for Gerontological Psychiatry, Boston, Massachusetts.

————, (1985b).   Parent care as a normative family stress.   *The Gerontologist,* 25:19–29.

Brody, E. M., C. Hoffman, M. H. Kleban and C. B. Schoonover. 1989.   Caregiving daughters and their local siblings: Perceptions, strains and interactions.   *The Gerontologist,* 29(4):529–538.

Brody, E. M., P. T. Johnsen, M. C. Fulcomer and A. M. Lang. 1983. Women's changing roles and help to elderly parents: Attitudes of three generations of women.   *Journal of Gerontology,* 38(5):597–607.

Brody, E. M., S. J. Litvin, C. Hoffman and M. H. Kleban. 1992. Differential effects of daughters' marital status on their parent care experiences.   *The Gerontologist,* 32(1):58–67.

Cantor, M. H. 1980.   The informal support system: its relevance in the lives of the elderly.   In *Aging and society* eds. E. Borgatta and N. McCluskey, 131–144. Beverly Hills, California: Sage.

————, 1983.   Strain among caregivers: A study of experience in the United States.   *The Gerontologist,* 23(6):597–604.

Cantor, M. H. and B. Hirshorn. 1988.   Intergenerational transfers within the family context-motivating factors and their implications for caregiving.   *Women and Health,* 14(3–4):39–51.

Chadiha, L. and N. Morrow-Howell. 1991.   Increasing the awareness of alzheimer's disease and assessing the unmet needs and strengths of African-American caregivers of elderly alzheimer's patients. Grant funded by the National Chapter of the Alzheimer's Association. Washington University, St. Louis, Missouri.

Chappell, N. 1990.   Aging and social care.   In. *Handbook of aging and the social sciences,* eds. R. Binstock and L. George.   San Diego, California: Academic Press.

Chatters, L. M. and R. J. Taylor. 1990.   Intergenerational support: the provision of assistance to parents by adult children.   In *Aging in black America.* eds. J. S. Jackson, L. M. Chatters and R. J. Taylor. Newbury Park, California: Sage.

Chenoweth, B. and B. Spencer. 1986.   Dementia: The experience of family caregivers.   *The Gerontologist,* 26(3):267–271.

Chesla, C., I. Martinson and M. Muwaswes. 1994.   Continuities and discontinuities in family members' relationships with alzheimer's patients.   *Family Relations,* 43:3–9.

Chiriboga, D. A., P. G. Weiler and K. Nielsen. 1988–1989. The stress of caregivers. *The Journal of Applied Social Sciences*, 13(1):118–141.

Choi, H. 1993. Cultural and noncultural factors as determinants of caregiver burden for the impaired elderly in South Korea. *The Gerontologist*, 33(1):8–15.

Cicirelli, V. G. 1981. Perceptions and feelings and behavior patterns: a basis for helping behavior. In *Helping elderly parents: The role of adult children*, V. G. Cicirelli, 19–30. Boston, Massachusetts: Auburn House Publishing Company.

————, 1983. Adult children's attachment and helping behavior to elderly parents: A path model. *Journal of Marriage and the Family*, 45:815–825.

————, 1984. Marital disruption and adult children's perception of their siblings' help to elderly parents. *Family Relations*, 33:613–621.

————, 1993. Attachment and obligation as daughters' motives for caregiving behavior and subsequent effect on subjective burden. *Psychology and Aging*, 8(2):144–155.

Clark, N. M. and W. Rakowski. 1983. Family caregivers of older adults: Improving helping skills. *The Gerontologist*, 23(6):637–642.

Cohen, J. 1960. A coefficient of agreement for nominal scales. *Educational and PsychologicalMeasurement*, 20(1):37–46.

Cohen, J. and P. Cohen. 1983. *Applied multiple regression/correlation analysis for the behavioral sciences*. New York: Halstead.

Cohen, D. and C. Eisdorfer. 1988. Dperession in family members caring for a relative with alzheimer's disease. *Journal of American Geriatrics Society*, 36:885–889.

Compton, B. R. and B. Galaway. 1979. *Social work processes*. Homewood, Illinois: The Dorsey Press.

Coward, R. T. and J. W. Dwyer. 1990. The association of gender, sibling network composition and patterns of parent care by adult children. *Research on Aging*,12(2):158–181.

Coward, R. T. and J. W. Dwyer. 1992. Gender and family care of the elderly. Research gaps and opportunities. In *Gender, families and elder care*, eds. J. W. Dwyer and R. T. Coward, 151–162. Newbury Park, California: Sage Publications.

Coward, R. T., C. Horne and J. W. Dwyer. 1992. Demographic perspectives on gender and family caregiving. In *Gender, families and elder care*, eds. J. W. Dwyer and R. T. Coward, 18–33. Newbury Park, California: Sage Publications.

Cox, C. 1993. Service needs and interests: a comparison of African-American and White caregivers seeking alzheimer's assistance. *The American Journal of Alzheimer's Care and Related Disorders and Research*, May/June:33–41.

Cox, C. and M. J. Verdieck. 1994. Factors affecting the outcomes of hospitalized dementia patients: from home to hospital to discharge. *The Gerontologist*, 34(4):497–504.

Cox, E. O., R. J. Parsons and P. J. Kimboko. 1988. Social services and intergenerational caregivers: issues for social work. *Social Work*, 430–434.

Creasy, G. L., B. J. Myers, M. J. Epperson and J. Taylor. 1990. Couples with an elderly parent with alzheimer's disease: perceptions of familial relationships. *Psychiatry*, 53:44–51.

Crossman, L., C. London and C. Barry. 1981. Older women caring for disabled spouses: A model for supportive services. *The Gerontologist*, 21(5):464–470.

Crouch, M. A. 1987. Role reversal of the elderly and their middle-aged children: emotional fusion across the life cycle. *Family Community Health*, 9(4):65–76.

Cutrona, C. E. 1986. Objective determinants of perceived social support. *Journal of Personality and Social Psychology*, 50(2):349–355.

Dawson, D., G. Hendershot and J. Fulton. 1987. Aging in the 80's: functional limitations of individuals age 65 and older. *Advance Data*, 133. Washington, D.C.: National Center for Health Statistics.

Doress-Worters, P. B. 1994. Adding elder care to women's multiple roles: a critical review of the caregiver stress and multiple roles literature. *Sex Roles*, 31(9/10):597–616.

Doty, P. 1986. Family care of the elderly: the role of public policy.
The Milbank Quarterly, 64(1):34–75.

Douglass, R. L. 1983. Domestic neglect and abuse of the elderly:
Implications for research and service. *Family Relations*, 32:395–
402.

Dowd, J. J. 1975. Aging as an exchange: a preface to theory. *Journal
of Gerontology*, 30:584–594.

Draughn, P. S., V. R. Tiller, S. A. McKellar and H. Dunaway. 1995.
Cost and need for caregiving of non-institutionalized elderly.
Poster presentation at National Council on Family Relations,
Portland, Oregon.

Eagles, J. M., A. Craig, F. Rawlinson, D. B. Restall, J. A. G. Beattie
and J. A. O. Besson. 1987. The psychological well-being of
supporters of the demented elderly. *British Journal of Psychiatry*,
150:293–298.

Eggert, G., C. Granger, R. Morris and S. Pendleton. 1977. Caring for
the patient with long-term disability. *Geriatrics*, 32:102–114.

Fatheringham, J., M. Skelton and B. Hoddinott. 1972. The effects on
the families of the presence of a mentally retarded child. *Canadian
Psychiatric Association Journal*, 17:283–289.

Finley, N. J., D. Roberts and B. F. Banahan. 1988. Motivators and
inhibitors of attitudes of filial obligation toward aging parents. *The
Gerontologist*, 28(1):73–78.

Fiore, J., J. Becker and D. B. Coppel. 1983. Social network
interactions: A buffer or a stress. *American Journal of Community
Psychology*, 11(4):423–439.

Fox, J. 1991. *Regression diagnostics*. Beverly Hills, California: Sage
Publications.

Gallo, J. J. 1990. The effect of social support on depression in
caregivers of the elderly. *The Journal of Family Practice*,
30(4):430–440.

George, L. K. 1986. Caregiver burdens: Conflict between norms of
reciprocity and solidarity. In *Elder abuse: Conflict in the family*,
eds. K. Pillemer and R. Wolf, 67–92). Dover, Massachusetts:
Auburn House.

George, L. K. and L. P. Gwyther. 1986. Caregiver well-being: A multidimensional examination of family caregivers of demented adults. *The Gerontologist*, 26(3):253–259.

Given, C. W., C. E. Collins and B. A. Given. 1988. Sources of stress among families caring for relatives with alzheimer's disease. *Nursing Clinics of North America*, 23(1):69–82.

Goldstein, V., G. Regnery and E. Wellin. 1981. Caretaker role fatigue. *Nursing Outlook*, 24–30.

Goode, W. J. 1960. A theory of role strain. *American Sociological Review*, 25:483–496.

Greene, J. G., R. Smith, M. Gardiner and G. C. Timbury. 1982. Measuring behavioural disturbance of elderly demented patients in the community and its effect on relatives: A factor analytic study. *Age and Aging*, 11:121–126.

Guberman, N., Maheu, P. and Maille, C. 1992. Women as family caregivers: Why do they care? *The Gerontologist*, 32(5):607–617.

Hagestad, G. O. 1994. Women and grandparents as kinkeepers. In *Aging Concepts and Controversies*, ed. H.R. Moody, 149–152. Thousand Oaks, California: Pine Forge Press.

Haley, W.E., R. P. Collins, V. G. Wadley, L. E. Harrell and D. L. Roth. 1992. Psychological and health symptoms among black and white dementia caregivers. Poster Presentation, American Psychological Association, Washington, D.C.

Hamon, R. R. 1988. Filial responsibility expectation among adult Children-older parent pairs. Paper presented at the 41st Annual Meeting of the Gerontological Society of America, San Francisco, California.

Hamon, R. R. and R. Blieszner. 1990. Filial responsibility expectations among adult child-older parent pairs. *Journal of Gerontology*, 45(3):P110–P112.

Hanson, S. L., W. J. Sauer and W. C. Seelbach. 1983. Racial and cohort variations in filial responsibility norms. *The Gerontologist*, 23(6):626–631.

Haug, M. R. 1973. Social class measurement and women's occupational roles. *Social Forces*, 52:86–98.

Heider, F. *The psychology of interpersonal relations*. New York: Wiley.

Hollingshead, A. B. 1957. *Two factor index of social position.* New Haven, Connecticut: Author.

————, 1975. *Four factor index of social status.* New Haven, Connecticut.

Hooyman, N. R. 1989. Changing sex roles in relation to care of the elderly. Paper presented at the National Association of Social Workers National Conference, San Francisco, California.

Hooyman, N. R. and Ryan, R. 1987. Women as caregivers of the elderly: Catch-22 dilemma. In *The trapped woman*, eds. J. Figueira-McDonough and R. Sarri, 143–171. Newbury Park, California: Sage Publications.

Horowitz, A. 1985a. Family caregiving to the frail elderly. In *Annual review of gerontology and geriatrics*, 5, ed. C. Eisdorfer. New York: Springer.

————, 1985b. Sons and daughters as caregivers to older parents: Differences in role performance and consequences. *The Gerontologist*, 25(6):612–617.

Horowitz, A. and Shindelman, L. W. 1983. Reciprocity and affection: Past influences on current caregiving. *Journal of Gerontological Social Work*, 5(3):5–20.

Houlihan, J. P. 1987. Families caring for frail and demented elderly: A review of selected findings. *Family Systems Medicine*, 5(3):344–356.

Houser, B. B., S. L. Berkman and P. Bardsley. 1985. Sex and birth order differences in filial behavior. *Sex Roles*, 13(11/12):641–651.

Hoyert, D. L. and M. M. Seltzer. 1992. Factors related to the well-being and life activities of family caregivers. *Family Relations*, 41:74–81.

Ikels, C. 1983. The caretaker selection process. *Research on Aging*, 5(4):497–509.

Ingersoll-Dayton, B. and T. C. Antonucci. 1988. Reciprocal and nonreciprocal social support: Contrasting sides of intimate relationships. *Journal of Gerontology*, 43(3):S65–S73.

Johnson, C. L. 1983. Dyadic family relations and social support. *The Gerontologist*, 23(4):377–383.

Jones, D. A. and N.J. Vetter. 1984. A survey of those who care for the elderly at home: Their problems and their needs. *Social Sciences Medicine*, 19(5):511–514.

Kahana, E. and R. Young, R. 1991. Clarifying the caregiving paradigm. In Aging and caregiving theory, research and policy, eds. D.E. Biegel and A. Blum, 76–97. Newbury Park, California: Sage Publications.

Karpel, M. A. and E. S. Strauss. 1983. *Family evaluation*. New York: Gardner Press, Inc.

Kelley, H. H. 1973. The processes of causal attribution. *American Psychologist*, 28, 107–128.

Kinney, J. M. and M. A. P. Stephens. 1989a. Caregiving hassles scale: Assessing the daily hassles of caring for a family member with dementia. *The Gerontologist*, 29(3):328–332.

———, 1989b. Hassles and uplifts of giving care to a Family member with dementia. *Psychology and Aging*, 4(4):402–408.

Kirschner, C. 1985. Social sork practice with the aged and their families: A systems approach. *Journal of Gerontological Social Work*, 55–69.

Kivett, V. R. and M. P. Anderson. 1984. Filial expectations, association, and helping as a function of number of children among older rural-transition parents. *Journal of Gerontology*, 33:109–125.

Kosberg, J. I. and R. E. Cairl. 1986. The cost of care index: A case management tool for screening informal care providers. *The Gerontologist*, 26(3):273–278.

Kruskal, J. B. 1968. Transformations of data. *International encyclopedia of the social sciences*, 182–193). New York: Macmillan.

Lang, A. M. and E. M. Brody. 1983. Characteristics of middle-aged daughters and help to their elderly mothers. *Journal of Marriage and the Family*, 45:193–202.

Lawton, M. P., D. Rajagopal, E. Brody and M. H. Kleban. 1992. The dynamics of caregiving for a demented elder among black and white families. *Journal of Gerontology*, 47(4):S156–S164.

Lazarus, R. S. and S. Folkman. 1984. Stress, appraisal and coping. New York: Springer.

Lee, G. R. 1980. Kinship in the 70's: A decade review of research and theory. *Journal of Marriage and the Family*, 42:193–204.

———, 1985. Theoretical perspectives on social networks. In *Social support networks and the care of the elderly*, eds. W. J. Sauer and R. T. Coward, 21–37. New York: Springer Publishing Company.

Lewis, F. M. and L. H. Daltroy. 1990. How causal explanations influence health behavior: Attribution theory. In *Health behavior and health education: Theory, research and practice*, eds. K. Glanz, F. M. Lewis and B. K. Rimer, 92–114. San Francisco, California: Josey-Bass Publishers.

Loomis, L. S. and A. Booth. 1995. Multigenerational caregiving and well-being: The myth of the beleaguered sandwich generation. *Journal of Family Issues*, 16(2):131–148.

Mancini, J. A. and R. Blieszner. 1989. Aging parents and adult children: Research themes in intergenerational relations. *Journal of Marriage and the Family*, 51:275–290.

Marks, S. R. 1977. Multiple roles and role strain: some notes on human energy, time and commitment. *American Sociological Review*, 42:921–936.

Masciocchi, C., A. Thomas and T. Moeller. 1984. Support for the impaired elderly: A challenge for family care-givers. In *Independent aging: Family and social system perspectives*, eds. W. H. Quinn and G. A. Hughston, 115–132. Rockville, Maryland: Aspen Publications.

Mason, C. A. and G. Kalton. 1972. *Survey methods and social investigation*. New York: Basic Books, Inc.

Matthews, S.H. and T. T. Rosner. 1988. Shared filial responsibility: The family as the primary caregiver. *Journal of Marriage and the Family*, 50:185–195.

Matthews, S. H., J. E. Wekner and P. J. Delaney. 1989. Relative contributions of help by employed and nonemployed sisters to their elderly parents. *Journal of Gerontology*, 44(1):S36–S44.

Midlarsky, E. 1994. Altruism through the life course. In *Family caregiving across the lifespan*, eds. E. Kahana, D. E. Biegel and M. L. Wykle, 69–95. Thousand Oaks, California: Sage Publications.

Miller, B. and L. Cafasso. 1992. Gender differences in caregiving: Fact or artifact? *The Gerontologist*, 32(4):498–507.

Miller, B. and A. Montgomery. 1990. Family caregivers and limitations in social activities. *Research on Aging*, 12(1):72–93.

Mitchell, J. and J. C. Register. 1984. An exploration of family interaction with the elderly by race, socioeconomic status, and residence. *The Gerontologist*, 24(1):48–54.

Montgomery, R. J. V. 1992. Gender differences in patterns of child-parent caregiving relationships. In *Gender, families and eldercare* J. W. Dwyer and R. T. Coward, 65–83. Newbury Park, California: Sage Publications.

Montgomery, R. J. V., J. G. Gonyea and N. R. Hooyman. 1985. Caregiving and the experience of subjective and objective burden. *Family Relations*, 34:19–26.

Montgomery, R. J. V. and B. A. Hirshorn. 1991. Current and future family help with long term care needs of the elderly. *Research on Aging*, 13(2): 171–204.

Montgomery, R. J. V., D. E. Stull and E. F. Borgatta. 1985b. Measurement and the analysis of burden. *Research on Aging*, 7(11): 137–152.

Moody, H. R. 1994. Should Families Provide For Their Own? In *Aging concepts and controversies*, ed. H R. Moody, 127–135. Thousand Oaks, California: Pine Forge Press.

Morris, J. C., A. Heyman, R. C. Mohs, J. P. Hughes, G. van Belle, G. Fillenbaum, E. D. Mellits, C. Clark and the CERAD investigators. 1989. The consortium to establish a registry for alzheimer's disease (CERAD). Part I. *Neurology*, 39:1159–1165.

Morrison, B. J. 1995. A research and policy agenda on predictors of institutional placement among minority elderly. *Journal of Gerontological Social Work*, 24 (1/2):17–28.

Morrow-Howell, N. 1994. The *M* word: Multicollinearity in multiple regression. *Social Work Research and Abstracts*, 18(4):247–251.

Morycz, R. K. 1985. Caregiving strain and the desire to institutionalize family members with alzheimer's disease: Possible predictors and model development. *Research on Aging*, 7(3):329–361.

Morycz, R., J. Malloy and P. Martz. 1987. Racial differences in family burden: Clinical implications for social work. *Journal of Gerontological Social Work*, 10:133–154.

Moser, C. A. and G. Kalton. 1972. *Survey methods in social investigation*. New York: Basic Books, Inc.

Mui, A. C. Y. 1990. *Caregiver strain among black and white daughter caregivers: A role theory perspective*. Ph.D. diss., Washington University, St. Louis, Missouri.

————, 1992. Caregiver strain among black and white daughter caregivers: A role theory perspective. *The Gerontologist*, 32(2):203–212.

Mutran, E. 1985. Intergenerational family support among blacks and whites: Response to culture or to socioeconomic differences. *Journal of Gerontology*, 40(3):382–389.

National Center for Health Statistics 1975. *Vital statistics of the U.S., 1973 life tables*. Rockville, Maryland: U.S. Government Printing Office.

National Center for Health Statistics 1987a. *Health/United States*. Washington, D.C.: Public Health Service, CDC, National Center for Health Statistics.

National Center for Health Statistics 1987b. *Public Health Service. Vital Statistics of the United States, 1987, Volume 1. Natality* (DHHS Publication No. PHS 89–100). Washington, D.C.: Government Printing Office.

Neufeld, A. and M. Harrison. 1992. Reciprocity in social support and the invisible work of caregiving. Presentation at the National Council on Family Relations, Orlando, Florida.

Noelker, L. S. and D. M. Bass. 1989. Home care for elderly persons: Linkages between formal and informal caregivers. *Journal of Gerontology*, 44(2):S63–S70.

Noelker, L. S. and G. Shaffer. 1986. Care networks—how they form and change. *Generations:* 62–64.

Novak, M. and C. Guest. 1989. Caregiver response to alzheimer's disease. *International Journal of Aging and Human Development*, 28(1):67–79.

Oberst, M. T., S. E. Thomas, K. A. Gass and S. E. Ward. 1989. Caregiving demands and appraisal of stress among family caregivers. *Cancer Nursing*, 12(4):209–215.

O'Connor, D.W., P. A. Pollitt, M. Roth, C. P. B. Brook and B. B. Reiss. 1990. Problems reported by relatives in a community study of dementia. *British Journal of Psychiatry*, 156:835-841.

Older Women's League. 1989. Failing America's caregivers: A status report on women who care. Washington, D.C.

Orlinsky, D. E. and K. I. Howard. 1978. The relation of process to outcome in psychotherapy. In *Handbook of psychotherapy and behavior change: An empirical analysis*, eds. S. L. Garfield and A. E. Bergin, 283-329. New York: John Wiley and Sons.

Orodenker, S. Z. 1990. Family caregiving in a changing society: The effects of employment on caregiver stress. *Family Community Relations*, 12(4):58-70.

Ory, M. G., T. F. Williams, M. Emr, B. Lebowitz, P. Rabins, J. Salloway, R. Sluss-Radbaugh, E. Wolff and S. Zarit. 1985. Families, informal supports and alzheimer's disease. *Research on Aging*, 7(4):623-644.

Pagano, R. P. 1981. *Understanding statistics in the behavioral sciences* (Third edition). St. Paul, Minnesota: West Publishing Company.

Parsons, R. J. and E. O. Cox. 1989. Family mediation in elder caregiving decisions: an empowerment intervention. *Social Work*, 34(2):122-126.

Pearlin, L. 1992. Caregiving: the unexpected career. Paper presented at the Social Policies and Research on Human Values Conference, St. Louis, Missouri.

Pearlin, L. I., J. T. Mullan, S. J. Semple and M. M. Skaff. 1990. Caregiving and the stress process: An overview of concepts and their measures. *The Gerontologist*, 30(5):583-594.

Pearlin, L. I. and C. Schooler. 1978. The structure of coping. *Journal of Health and Social Behavior*, 19:2-21.

Pearlman, D. N. and W. H. Crown. 1992. Alterantive sources of social support and their impacts on institutional risk. *The Gerontologist*, 32(4):527-535.

Pearson, J., S. Verma and C. Nellett. 1988. Elderly psychiatric patient status and caregiver perceptions as predictors of caregiver burden. *The Gerontologist*, 28(1):79-83.

Pedhazur, E. J. 1982. *Multiple regression in behavioral research.* Fort Worth, Texas: Holt, Rinehart and Winston, Inc.

Penning, M. J. 1990. Receipt of assistance by elderly people: Hierarchical selection and task specificity. *The Gerontologist,* 30(2):220–227.

Phillips, L. R. and V. F. Rempusheski. 1986. Caring for the frail elderly at home: Toward a theoretical explanation of the dynamics of poor quality family caregiving. *Advances in Nursing Science,* 8(4):62–84.

Pietromonaco, P. R., J. Manis and K. Frohardt-Lane. 1986. Psychological consequences of multiple roles. *Psychology of Women Quarterly,* 10:373–382.

Poulshock, S. W. and G. Deimling. 1984. Families caring for elders in residence: Issues in the measurement of burden. *Journal of Gerontology,* 39:230–239.

Pratt, C. C., L. L. Jones, H. Shin and A. J. Walker. 1989. Autonomy and decision making between single older women and their caregiving daughters. *The Gerontologist,* 29(6):792–797.

Pratt, C. C. and A. Kethley. 1988. Aging and family caregiving in the future: Implications for education and policy. *Educational Gerontology,* 14:567–576.

Pratt, C., V. Schmall and S. Wright. 1987. Ethical concerns of family caregivers to dementia patients. *The Gerontologist,* 27(5):632–638.

Pratt, C., V. Schmall and S. Wright. 1986. Family caregivers and dementia. *Social Casework: The Journal of Contemporary Social Work,* 119–124.

Proctor, E. K., N. Morrow-Howell. and L. Chadiha. 1990. Adequacy of home care for chronically ill elderly. Research Grant funded by Agency for Health Care Policy and Research (HS 06 406–01). Washington University, St. Louis, Missouri.

Pruchno, R. A. 1990. The effects of help patterns on the mental health of spouse caregivers. *Research on Aging,* 12(1):57–71.

Quinn, W. H. 1984. Autonomy, interdependence and developmental delay in older generations of the family. In *Independent aging: Family and social system perspectives,* eds. W. H. Quinn and G. A. Hughston, 21–34. Rockville, Maryland: Aspen Publications.

Rabins, P. V., N. L. Mace. and M. J. Lucas. 1982. The impact of dementia on the family. *Journal of the American Medical Association*, 248(3):333–335.

Rakowski, W. and N. M. Clark. 1985. Future outlook, caregiving and care-receiving in the family context. *The Gerontologist*, 19(6):586–593.

Rathbone-McCuan, E. E., N. Hooyman. and A. E. Fortune. 1985. Social supports for the frail elderly. In *Social support networks and the care of the elderly*, eds. W. J. Sauer and C. T. Coward, 234–247. New York: Springer Publishing Company.

Redinbaugh, E. M., R. C. MacCaullum and J. K. Kiecolt-Glaser. 1995. Recurrent syndromal depression in caregivers. *Psychology and Aging*, 10(3):358–368.

Reece, D., T. Walz. and H. Hageboeck. 1983. Intergenerational care providers of non-institutionalized frail elderly: characteristics and consequences. *Journal of Gerontological Social Work*, 5(3):21–34.

Reed, B. R., A. A. Stone and J. M. Neale. 1990. Effects of caring for a demented relative on elders' life events and appraisals. *The Gerontologist*, 30(2):200–205.

Robinson, B. C. 1983. Validation of a caregiver stress index. *Journal of Gerontology*, 38(3):344–348.

Robinson, B. C. 1993. Telephone conversation with the author.

Robinson, B. and M. Thurnher. 1979. Taking care of aged parents: A family cycle transition. *The Gerontologist*, 19(6):586–593.

Rowe, J. and R. Kahn. 1987. Human aging: Usual and successful. *Science*, 237:143–149.

Rubio, D. M. 1992. *Transformations for a linear fit*. Working paper. Washington University, St. Louis, Missouri.

SAS Institute, Inc. 1988. SAS/STAT User's Guide, Release 6.03 Edition. Cary, N.C.: SAS Institute.

Sauer, W. J. and R. T. Coward. 1985. The role of social support networks in the care of the elderly. In *Social support networks and the care of the elderly*, eds. W. J. Sauer and R. T. Coward, 3–20. New York: Springer Publishing Company.

Scharlach, A. E. 1987. Role-strain in mother-daughter relationships in later life. *The Gerontologist*, 27(5):627–631.

Schulz, R. 1990. Theoretical perspectives on caregiving. Concepts, variables, and methods. In *Aging and caregiving: Theory, research and policy*, eds. D. E. Biegel and A. Blum, 27–52. Newbury Park, California: Sage Publications.

Scott, J. P., K. A. Roberto and J. T. Hutton. 1986. Families of alzheimer's victims: Family support to the caregivers. *Journal of American Geriatrics Society*, 34:348–354.

Seelbach, W. C. 1984. Filial responsibility and the care of aging family members. In *Independent aging: family and social system perspectives*, eds. W. H. Quinn and G. A. Hughston, 92–105. Rockville, Maryland: Aspen Publications.

Shanas, E. (1968). Old people in three industrial societies. New York: Atherton Press.

———, 1979a. The family as a social support system in old age. *The Gerontologist*, 19(2):69–174.

———, 1979b. Social myths as hypothesis: The case of the family relations of old people. *The Gerontologist*, 19(1):3–9.

Shellenberger, S., K. W. Couch and M. A. Drake. 1989. Elderly family members and their caregivers: Characteristics and development of the relationship. *Family Systems Medicine*, 7(3):317–322.

Sieber, S. D. 1974. Toward a theory of role accumulation. *American Sociological Review*, 39:567–578.

Skaff, M. and L. I. Pearlin. 1992. Caregiving: Role engulfment and the loss of self. *The Gerontologist*, 32(5):656–664.

Snyder, B. and K. Keefe. 1985. The umet needs of family caregivers for frail and disabled adults. *Social Work in Health Care*, 10(3):1–14.

Soldo, B.J. and J. Myllyluoma. 1983. Caregivers who live with dependent elderly. *The Gerontologist*, 23(6):605–611.

Spitze, G. and J. R. Logan. 1992. Helping as a component of parent-adult child relations. *Research on Aging*, 14(3):291–312.

Spitze, G., J. R. Logan, G. Joseph and E. Lee. 1994. Middle generation roles and the well-being of men and women. *Journal of Gerontology*, 49(3):S107–S116.

Spitze, G. and S. Miner. 1992. Gender differences in adult child contact among black elderly parents. *The Gerontologist,* 32(2):213–218.

Staight, P. R. and S. M. Harvey. 1990. Caregiver burden: A comparison between elderly women as primary caregivers and secondary caregivers for their spouses. *Journal of Gerontological Social Work,* 15(1/2): 89–104.

Steinmetz, S. K. 1988. Elder abuse by family caregivers: Processes and intervention strategies. *Contemporary Family Therapy,* 10(4):256–271.

Stephens, M. A. P., V. K. Norris, J. M. Kinney, S. W. Ritchie and R. C. Grotz. 1988. Stressful situations in caregiving: Relations between caregiver coping and well-being. *Psychology and Aging,* 3(2): 208–209.

Stoller, E. P. 1983. Parental caregiving by adult children. *Journal of Marriage and the Family,* 45:851–859.

————, 1990. Males as helpers: The role of sons, relatives, and friends. *The Gerontologist,* 30(2):228–235.

Stoller, E. P. and L. L. Earl. 1983. Help with activities of everyday life: Sources of support for the noninstitutionalized elderly. *The Gerontologist,* 23(1):64–70.

Stoller, E. P. and K. L. Pugliesi. 1989a. Other roles of caregivers: Competing responsibilities or supportive resources. *Journal of American Geriatrics Society,* 44(6):S231–S238.

————, 1989b. The transition to the caregiving role: A panel study of helpers of elderly people. *Research on Aging,* 11(3):213–230.

Stone, R., G. L. Cafferata and J. Sangl. 1987. Caregivers of the frail elderly: A national profile. *The Gerontologist,* 27(5):616–626.

Sudman, S. and N. M. Bradburn. 1982. *Asking questions: A practical guide to questionnaire design.* San Francisco, California: Josey-Bass Publishers.

Taylor, R. J. and L. M. Chatters. 1989. Family, friend, and church support networks of black Americans. In *Black adult development and aging,* ed. R. L. Jones, 245–271). Berkeley, California: Cobb and Henry Publishing.

Tennstedt, S. L., S. Crawford and J. B. McKinlay. 1993. Determining the pattern of community care: Is co-residence more important than caregiver relationship? *Journal of Gerontology*, 48(2):S74–S83.

Thompson, E. H., A. M. Futterman, D. Gallagher-Thompson, J. M. Rose and S. B. Lovett. 1993. Social support and caregiving burden in family caregivers of frail elders. *Journal of Gerontology*, 48(5):S245–S254.

Toseland, R. W. and C. M. Rossiter. 1989. Group interventions to support family caregivers: A review and analysis. *The Gerontologist*, 29(4):438–448.

Townsend, A. L. and S. W. Poulshock. 1986. Intergenerational perspectives on impaired elders' support networks. *Journal of Gerontology*, 41(1):101–109.

U.S. Department of Health and Human Services. 1988. Blessed-Roth Dementia Scale (DS). *Psychopharmacology Bulletin*, 24(4):705–708. Washington, D. C.

U.S. Select Committee on Aging. 1987. Exploding the myths: Caregiving in America (Comm. Pub. 99–611). Washington, D.C.: U.S. Government Printing Office.

Wagoner, B. and J. R. Bohannon. 1995. The psychological well-being of older adults. Poster presentation at National Council on Family Relations, Portland, Oregon.

Waldo, D. R. and H. C. Lazenby. 1984. Demographic characteristics and health care use and expenditures by the aged in the United States 1977–1984, *Health Care Financing Review*, 6(1).

Walker, A. J. and K. R. Allen. 1991. Relationships between caregiving daughters and their elderly mothers. *The Gerontologist*, 31(3):389–396.

Walker, A. J. and C. C. Pratt. 1991. Daughters' help to mothers: Intergenerational aid versus caregiving. *Journal of Marriage and the Family*, 53:3–12.

Walker, A. J., C. C. Pratt and L. Eddy. 1995. Informal caregiving to aging families: A critical review. *Family Relations*, 44:402–411.

Walker, A. J., C. C. Pratt and N. C. Oppy. 1992. Perceived reciprocity in family caregiving. *Family Relations*, 41:82–85.

Walker, A. J., C. C. Pratt and B. Wood. 1992. Perceived frequency of role conflict and relationship quality for caregiving daughters. Paper presented at the National Council on Family Relations. Orlando, Florida.

Ward, R. A. and G. Spitze. 1992. Consequences of parent-adult child coresidence. *Journal of Family Issues*, 13(4):553–572.

Weiss, R. S. 1974. The provisions of social relationships. In *Doing unto others*, Z. Rubin, 17–26. Englewood Cliffs, New Jersey: Prentice-Hall, Inc.

Wentowski, G. J. 1981. Reciprocity and the coping strategies of older people: Cultural dimensions of network building. *The Gerontologist*, 21(6):600–609.

Wolman, B.B. 1989. *Dictionary of behavioral science*. San Diego, California: Academic Press, Inc.

Worcester, M. I. and M. P. Quayhagen. 1983. Correlates of caregiving satisfaction: Prerequisites to elder home care. *Research in Nursing and Health*, 6:61–67.

Young, R. F. and E. Kahana. 1989. Specifying caregiver outcomes: Gender and relationship aspects of caregiving strain. *The Gerontologist*, 29(5):660–666.

Zarit, S. H., K. E. Reever and J. Bach-Peterson. 1980. Relatives of the impaired elderly: Correlates of feelings of burden. *The Gerontologist*, 20(6):649–655.

Zarit, S. H., P. A. Todd and J. M. Zarit. 1986. Subjective burden of husbands and wives as caregivers: A longitudinal study. *The Gerontologist*, 26(3):260–266.

APPENDIX A
Caregiver Strain Measures

SCALE	DESCRIPTION	SAMPLE	RELIABILITY/VALIDITY/ COMMENT
Relatives' Stress Scale (1982) Greene, Smith, Gardiner and Timbury	20-item likert scale	38 caregivers of demented elders	Test-re-test reliability r = .85 Mean stress level 1.8 (scale of 0–4)

Appendix A (cont'd)
Caregiver Strain Measures

SCALE	DESCRIPTION	SAMPLE	RELIABILITY/VALIDITY/COMMENT
Caregiving Hassles Scale (1989) Kinney and Stephens	42-item scale with 5 sub-scales of hassles of caregiving in last week: ADL (9); IADL(7); cognitive (9); behavior (12); and social network (5)	60 primary caregivers of community-dwelling family members with Alzheimer's Disease	24-hr test-retest reliability: full scale .83; range: .66–.87 Internal consistency (Cronbach's alpha: full scale .91; range: 74–.89 Subscale intercorrelations: -.01–.67 Construct validity: full scale range: -.18–.51 Comments: *Behavior subscale has highest internal consistency *Behavior and ADL subscales has strongest test-retest reliability *Support network subscale has weakest test-re-test reliability *Low association between ADL hassles and well-being *Long duration of caregiving may result in routinized ADL care

Appendix A (cont'd)
Caregiver Strain Measures

SCALE	DESCRIPTION	SAMPLE	RELIABILITY/VALIDITY/COMMENT
Cost of Care Index (1986) Kosberg and Kairl	20-item likert scale with 5 dimensions: personal and social restrictions; physical and emotional health; value; provocateur and economic (4 items each)	83 caregivers of elder family members from education program, AD support group or MA recipients	Factor analysis: coefficient alpha = .91 for internal reliability Subscale intercorrelations: strong between all dimensions except Value which remains independent. Comments: *High intercorrelations between subscale
Impact Scale(1984) Poulshock and Deimling	34-item scale with 2 factors: elder-caregiver and caregiver-family relationship (11) and social activity restriction (23)	614 families stratified by geographic area; race and generational configuration	Factor analysis results: Factor 1 range .46–.75; Factor 2 range .50–.70 52% report 2+ areas of negative impact 68% report 2+ areas of activity restriction Comments: *Subscales are too general; limits reliability

Appendix A (cont'd)
Caregiver Strain Measures

SCALE	DESCRIPTION	SAMPLE	RELIABILITY/VALIDITY/COMMENT
Appraisal of Caregiving Scale (1989) Oberst, Thomas, Gass and Ward	53-item likert scale with 4 dimensions: harm/loss (15); threat (15); challenge (15); and benign (8)	47 family caregivers of adults in radiotherapy for cancer	Inter-rater reliability (6 clinicians) classified 51 of 53 items correctly Subscale intercorrelations .32–.64) Interitem correlations: Harm/loss .31; Threat .41; Challenge .14; Benign .30; Internal consistency: Harm/loss .87; Threat .91; Challenge .72; Benign .77 Comments: *Results may be artifact of time spent in caregiving *High intercorrelations between harm/loss and threat subscales leads to overlapping constructs *High intercorrelations between challenge and benign subscales due to lack of clarity

SCALE	DESCRIPTION	SAMPLE	RELIABILITY/VALIDITY/COMMENT
Caregiver Load Scale (1989) Oberst et al	10-item likert scale of caregiver tasks	See above	Interitem correlation .40 Internal consistency .87
Burden Scale (1990) Pruchno	17-item scale measuring frequency of feelings of burden in past month	315 spouse caregivers of elders with AD or related disorder	Internal consistency (coefficient alpha) = .89 Correlation with Uplift Scale (developed for this study) = -.42 Comments: * Adequate construct validity between burden and uplift scales
Caregiver Strain Index (1983) Robinson	13-item dichotomous scale with 3 strain areas: ex-patient characteristics; perception of caregiving; and emotional status	85 primary caregivers of elders discharged from the hospital with heart disease or hip fracture	Internal consistency (Cronbach's alpha) = .86 Construct validity: 1) Ex-patient characteristics and caregiver strain index range:.46–.39 2) subjective perceptions of caregiving and caregiver emotional status range: .43–.67

Appendix A (cont'd)
Caregiver Strain Measures

SCALE	DESCRIPTION	SAMPLE	RELIABILITY/VALIDITY/COMMENT
Caregiver Stress Scale (1983) Worcester and Quayhagen	Likert scale with 3 situational stress subscales: medical-psychological; psychological-behavioral; and environmental-personal	19 current caregivers living with elder and 29 past co-resident caregivers of elders now in nursing home	Internal consistency (coefficient alpha): medical-psychological .80 psychological-behavioral .83 environmental-personal .82
Burden Inventory (1980) Zarit, Reever and Bach-Peterson	29-item self-report likert inventory	29 primary caregivers of community-dwelling demented family members	Not reported

APPENDIX B
Caregiving Strain Studies

STRAIN FACTORS	AUTHOR	YEAR	DEPENDENT VARIABLE	FINDINGS
Elder Factors: Number of Memory/Behavior Problems and Changes	Baillie Norbeck Barnes	1988	Psychological distress	Elder mental status (and years of caregiving) only 2 significant predictors of psychological distress.
	Barusch Spaid	1987	Burden	Number of memory/behavior problems contributed 14% of variance in burden.
	Eagles Craig Rawlinson Restall Beattie Besson	1987	Psychological Well-being and Stress	Co-resident caregivers of demented elders experienced higher levels of stress than non-demented elder caregivers which escalates with the severity of dementia.

Appendix B (cont'd)
Caregiver Strain Studies

STRAIN FACTORS	AUTHOR	YEAR	DEPENDENT VARIABLE	FINDINGS
	Kinney Stephens	1989	Caregiving Hassles and Uplifts	Elder social withdrawal accounted for 22.4% of variance and inappropriate behavior contributed 23% of variance in behavior hassles. For cognitive hassles, inappropriate behavior = 15% and social withdrawal = 13.4% of variance. Inappropriate behavior contributed 7% of variance in practical hassles.
	Pratt Schmall Wright	1985 1986	Burden and Coping Strategies	Poor patient mental status leads to higher stress. Caregiver burden scores related to 3 internal coping strategies (confidence in problem solving, reframing and passivity) and 2 external strategies (spiritual and extended family support).
	Zarit Todd Zarit	1986	Burden (subjective)	Subjective burden found over time on the variable related to patient behavior problems.
Illness Severity and Type	Bass Tausig Noelker	1988- 1989	Strain	High strain reported at Time 1 continues to be present at Time 2 (54% of variance in strain).

Appendix B (cont'd)
Caregiver Strain Studies

STRAIN FACTORS	AUTHOR	YEAR	DEPENDENT VARIABLE	FINDINGS
	George Gwyther	1986	Stress Symptom	The more severe the symptoms, the higher the stress symptom (along with lower health scores and leisure time).
	Kinney Stephens	1989	Caregiving Hassles and Uplifts	Degree of physical limitations contributed 17.1% of variance to ADL hassles.
	Novak Guest	1989	Burden	Moderately significant correlation (.38) between severity of dementia and burden. Severity of dementia accounted for 14% of variance in burden.
	Oberst Thomas Gass Ward	1989	Caregiver Appraisal of Stress	Perceived caregiver load is a function of caregiver illness characteristics.
	Pearson Verma Nellett	1988	Caregiver Perception of Burden	Patient functional status and disruptive behavior contributed most to caregiver perception of burden, but not cognitive impairment alone.

Appendix B (cont'd)
Caregiver Strain Studies

STRAIN FACTORS	AUTHOR	YEAR	DEPENDENT VARIABLE	FINDINGS
	Poulshock Deimling	1984	Burden	Moderate to strong empirical link between elder impairment characteristics and caregiver perception of burden and negative impact on elder-caregiver relationship.
Phase of Illness 1. Early Phase	Chenoweth Spencer	1986	Stress	Stress levels are highest in the early phase of a dementing illness.
	Novak Guest	1989	Burden	Stress levels are highest in the first year of caregiving for an elder with Alzheimer's Disease.
2. Middle Phase	Chiriboga Weiler Nielson	1988-1989	Stressors	Care demands (stressors) peak in mid-phases of caregiving for an elder with Alzheimer's Disease.
Caregiver Factors: Gender	Anthony-Bergstone Zarit Gatz	1988	Burden	Women report higher burden levels than men.
	Barusch Spaid	1989	Burden	Women report higher levels of burden due to: caregiver age (younger), patient care demands (higher), less use of formal/informal support and poorer coping responses.

Appendix B (cont'd)
Caregiver Strain Studies

STRAIN FACTORS	AUTHOR	YEAR	DEPENDENT VARIABLE	FINDINGS
	Brody Hoffman Kleban Schoonover	1989	Strain	Women report higher stress levels due to caregiving roles being rooted in traditional gender role expectations; therefore, women cannot always fulfill own expectations which leads to guilt and strain.
	Cantor	1983	Strain	In a 14-variable model (5 significant variables), gender is the fourth highest contributor to variance (2.7%).
	Kinney Stephens	1989	Caregiving Hassles and Uplifts	Gender (female) contributed 16.9% of variance in behavior and cognitive hassles.
	O'Connor Pollitt Roth Brook Reiss	1990	Burden	Women find "nurse" role more burdensome than men, but also assume the role earlier in the course of the illness than men do.
	Young Kahana	1989	Strain	Women report higher levels of burden (and role conflict, physical decline and mental health symptoms), but provide more care than men.

Appendix B (cont'd)
Caregiver Strain Studies

STRAIN FACTORS	AUTHOR	YEAR	DEPENDENT VARIABLE	FINDINGS
Age	Barusch Spaid	1989	Burden	Younger caregivers experience increased burden (10% of the variance in burden).
	Johnson	1983	Stress	Children (vs spouses) report higher stress levels.
	Jones Vetter	1984	Stress	Daughters (vs spouses) report higher stress levels.
Relationship to Elder	Anthony-Bergstone Zarit Gatz	1988	Psychological Distress	Wives are more vulnerable to psychological stress (even more than daughters).
	Creasy Myers Epperson Taylor	1990	Burden	In a study of couples, females (daughters and daughters-in-law) report higher levels of burden related to negative interactions with parents and husbands. Males are more stressed only when the elder is his parent.
	Horowitz	1985	Stress	Daughters more stressed than sons (less involved in caregiving and report fewer negative effects (loss of leisure time and family neglect).
	Johnson	1983	Stress	Adult children report stress more often than any other group.

STRAIN FACTORS	AUTHOR	YEAR	DEPENDENT VARIABLE	FINDINGS
	Jones Vetter	1984	Stress	Daughters report the most stress.
	O'Connor Pollitt Roth Brook Reiss	1990	Strain	Adult children report higher levels of strain than spouses.
	Young Kahana	1989	Burden	Adult children report high levels of burden/role conflict) with daughters reporting highest levels.
Attitude/ Perception Toward Caregiving	Cantor	1983	Strain	The more caregiver feels family is responsible and involvement is a positive value, the higher the strain level (contributed 6% of variance).
	Cicirelli	1993	Subjective burden	Level of caregiver obligation to the elder is related to increased subjective burden.
	Rakowski Clark	1985	Stress	Limited future outlook may exacerbate stress. Over 1/2 of the caregiver/dyads were congruent in the future outlook and stress.
	Robinson Thurnher	1979	Stress	Stress results from caregiver perception of caregiving as confining.

143

Appendix B (cont'd)
Caregiver Strain Studies

STRAIN FACTORS	AUTHOR	YEAR	DEPENDENT VARIABLE	FINDINGS
Health	Pratt Schmall Wright	1986	Burden	Caregivers with poorer health report higher burden scores (79% report caregiving negatively affected health).
Competing Roles	Orodenker	1990	Stress	Employed caregivers report significantly more stress than unemployed caregivers due to an inability to balance the roles and being forced to alter work schedules.
	Stoller Pugliesi	1989	Burden/ Psychological Stress	Other roles relate to burden when care needs are high (but are positively related to caregiver well-being).
Race	Lawton Rajagopal Brody Kleban	1992	Burden	African-American caregivers report lower levels of subjective burden than White caregivers. As traditional ideology levels increased, burden decreased.
Relationship Factors: Closeness and Affection	Cantor	1983	Strain	Degree of compatibility between caregiver and elder contributes approximately 3% of variance in burden (5th in a 14-variable model).

Appendix B (cont'd)
Caregiver Strain Studies

STRAIN FACTORS	AUTHOR	YEAR	DEPENDENT VARIABLE	FINDINGS
	Cicirelli	1993	Subjective Burden	Caregiver's feelings of attached are related to decreased levels of subjective burden.
	Cox Parsons Kimboko	1988	Burden	High levels of subjective burden relate to low levels of affection.
	Pratt Schmall Wright	1986	Burden	Burden scores are higher when caregiver and elder relationship was not close prior to caregiving.
	Scharlach	1987	Role Strain	Role strain is related to sense of role demand overload and to a lesser extent, perception of role inadequacy and employment status.
	Stoller Pugliesi	1989	Burden/ Psychological Stress	Caregiver assessment of relationship as positive results in less burden and fewer symptoms of psychological stress/depression.
Caregiving Arrangement Factors: Co-residence	Eagles, Craig Rawlinson Restall Beattie Besson	1987	Stress	Co-resident caregivers of demented elders experience more stress than caregivers of non-demented elders which escalates with severity of dementia.

Appendix B (cont'd)
Caregiver Strain Studies

STRAIN FACTORS	AUTHOR	YEAR	DEPENDENT VARIABLE	FINDINGS
	George Gwyther	1986	Stress Symptoms	Co-resident caregivers report highest level of stress symptoms and more psychotropic drug use and lowest level of affect and life satisfaction.
	Reece Walz Hageboeck	1983	6 impact areas: personal time; mental health; work; marriage; physical health; and spouse's work	Co-residence impacts more negatively than overall level of task involvement.
	Stoller Pugliesi	1989	Burden/ Psychological Stress	Co-residence is not predictive of burden, but did result in higher levels of psychological stress.
Amount and Type of Care Provided	Pratt Schmall Wright	1986	Burden	Burden scores are higher for caregivers reporting 10+ hours/day devoted to caregiving.

Appendix B (cont'd)
Caregiver Strain Studies

STRAIN FACTORS	AUTHOR	YEAR	DEPENDENT VARIABLE	FINDINGS
Tasks Performed	Montgomery Gonyea Hooyman	1985	Objective and Subjective Burden	Tasks that constrain the caregiver's time schedule and/or geographic location are best predictors of objective burden.
Social Support	Morycz Zarit Reever Bach-Peterson	1985 1980	Strain Burden	Less family support increases caregiver strain. The extent of burden is associated with available social supports (number of visitors to the house).
Duration of Caregiving	Baillie Norbeck Barnes	1988	Psychological Distress	More years of caregiving and higher levels of impaired elder mental status are the only two significant predictors of psychological distress.

APPENDIX C
Sample Source Description

Research Project	Authors	Date	Eligibility Criteria	Method of Date Collection	Size
Adequacy of Home Care for Chronically Ill Elderly (Care Plan Study)	Proctor Morrow-Howell Chadiha	1990	Community dwelling elderly patients (65 years and older) and their family caregivers	Personal and telephone interviews	38
Increasing the Awareness of AD and Assessing the Unmet Needs and Strengths of African-American Caregivers of Elderly Alzheimer's Patients	Chadiha Morrow-Howell	1992	Non-institutionalized African-American elders with indications of cognitive impairment and their family caregivers	Personal interviews	22
Memory and Aging Project Satellite	Berg Edwards	1992	Minority and medically underserved elders and family members	Personal interviews	13

APPENDIX D
Sample of Reasons for Caregiver Selection Responses
(N = 40)

Category #1: Request from family, elder, agency or court

1. "Father asked me to move back from California to care for her (mother); father not wanting the responsibility."
2. "Social worker called me and asked me."
3. "Partly my mother's decision. She just kind of gravitated to me, just like expecting me to be there."
4. "The courts decided. I was appointed by the courts. Court person gave his opinion after having been around all of us (family)."
5. "She came to my house and decided to stay."
6. "The state (Michigan) turned her over to her son. Her husband was working and he asked me if I would take care of her, so I have been taking care of her since 1987."
7. "I was an outside person to my Dad. I demanded he ask for my help. He asked someone else to ask me to help him."
8. "I was to move in with parents before. They had asked me to."

Category #2: No Other Alternatives

1. "I'm the only child; have no one else to do it."
2. "He had no where else to go. He had no one else. I'm the only daughter."
3. "I'm the only one. It's expected of me (by Dad)."
4. "I am an only child. There was no one else to do it."

5. "I am an only child. Her condition changed, so I went to get her. I'd have to take her or she would have been placed in a home. My family and I decided to take care of her."
6. "Sister called a meeting to say she needs help. Everyone said not me. I finally said I would take her. At first, I also said not me."
7. "I am the only one who decided that I would."
8. "Being the only child."
9. "Only child; I had no choice."
10. "Since she didn't have her own children, I was her baby. I've been there for her since 1979."
11. "Husband and I had an apartment. Having difficulty making it financially. Sisters had no room. One sister already a caregiver. We were the only ones, so we moved in with her."
12. "I'm the only child and my father died."
13. "I'm the only immediate living relative in St. Louis; a brother in California; only had phone contact."
14. "I have a brother (irresponsible) and a sister (doesn't get along with Mom), so I'm the only one."
15. "I'm an only child; he's all I've got and I'm all he's got."
16. "There was no choice. I was the only one."
17. "I'm an only child."
18. "I'm an only child and my parents were older when I was born. My parents are foreign-born and never adjusted to America, so I've always been doing things for them."

Category #3: Family Position

1. "I am the oldest daughter. I took an early retirement to take care of her. My sister and I talked about it and the decision was made that I would do it" (family position due to combination of availability and family decision).

2. "I am the oldest. My son is grown with a family and I was not working at the time" (family position due to availability).
3. "I am the youngest child. It fell on me. My older siblings are senior citizens and couldn't take care of him" (family position due to availability).
4. "I was the only one who could do it. I'm the oldest. Since I was born, it's been that way all my life" (family position due to family "rules").
5. "I'm the youngest. Before the CVA, it was always me and her together. They (family) promised to help, but didn't" (family position due to family culture/rules).

Category #4: Sense of Duty and Obligation

1. "Brother wasn't helping. Father asked me to look after Mom. I felt I should do it and my brother never offered."
2. "She's my mother and I felt I should do it. She took care of me and I wanted to return that."
3. "I was the most available (just lost job). I feel responsible. Why do we get assigned to these "things"? She's been there for me."
4. "Sister had no commitments. I do day care. We felt obligated."

Category #5: Other (Self-Decision)

1. "A self brought-on decision. Nothing that was discussed."
2. "This has been an on and off thing since I graduated from high school. I decided to do it on my own."
3. "My brother and I decided to do it ourselves. It's just the two of us."
4. "Brothers live up north. They help financially. Sisters help to a point. There was no one else. I'd have done it anyway. It's just my nature."

5. "We've always had a good relationship. I wasn't
        asked. I just picked it up. I could have called my
        ·brother (out of the country). I never felt forced.
        I just picked it up. A lot of how you react is based
        on what's going on in your life."

INDEX

157